CARVER
COUNTY
LIBRARY

**Supported by the
City Council and Economic
Development Commission of
Norwood Young America**

# Praise for *Free Marketing*

"It's obvious from reading this book that Jim Cockrum not only knows about marketing, but that he honestly cares about helping his readers succeed. Whether you're a seasoned Internet marketer or just getting started, Jim provides plenty of great ideas to improve your business."

—**Terry Gibbs**
**IWantCollectibles.com**

"Jim is a genius, but also a natural teacher. He has a heart for people. He has built a very successful business online and offline and doesn't mind sharing what he knows with others."

—**Rhea Perry**
**EducatingforSuccess.com**

*Free Marketing* is incisive and to the point. Real information any marketer can use today—and it's from one of the most trusted people on the Internet.

—**Skip McGrath**
**SkipMcGrath.com**

"Your book is unreal Jim. I can't read more. I have too much to do because of the first 22 pages! I've never read *anything* with so many actionable tips and so little fluff in my life."

—**John Jonas**
**JonasBlog.com**

# FREE MARKETING

## 101 LOW AND NO-COST WAYS

TO YOUR
GROW BUSINESS

ONLINE & OFF

## JIM COCKRUM

**WILEY**

John Wiley & Sons, Inc.

Published by John Wiley & Sons, Inc., Hoboken, New Jersey.
Published simultaneously in Canada.

For general information on our other products and services or for technical support, please contact our Customer Care Department within the United States at (800) 762-2974, outside the United States at (317) 572-3993 or fax (317) 572-4002.

Wiley also publishes its books in a variety of electronic formats. Some content that appears in print may not be available in electronic books. For more information about Wiley products, visit our website at www.wiley.com.

*Library of Congress Cataloging-in-Publication Data:*
Cockrum, Jim, 1969–
    Free marketing : 101 low and no-cost ways to grow your business, online and off / Jim Cockrum.
        p. cm.
    Includes index.
    ISBN 978-1-118-03471-2 (hardback); ISBN 978-1-118-12004-0 (ebk);
ISBN 978-1-118-12003-3 (ebk); ISBN 978-1-118-12002-6 (ebk)
    1. Marketing.   2. Branding (Marketing)   3. Internet marketing.
4. Corporate image.   I. Title.
    HF5415.C54237 2011
    658.8–dc22

                                                                2011014259

Printed in the United States of America.

10   9   8   7   6   5   4   3   2   1

*For Andrea*

# CONTENTS

## PART 7
## Get Creative with the Media

## PART 8
## Smartphones Are Taking Over the World

## PART 9
## Inch-Wide, Mile-Deep Marketing

## PART 10
## Video Is No Longer Optional

## PART 11
## Deliver Current Content Constantly

# PART 15
## Spoiled Prospects and Customers Are Loyal

# PART 16
## Powerful Marketing Partnerships

## PART 17
## Make Your Story Powerful

## PART 18
## Actually, You Are Selling *You*

## PART 19
## We Like to Buy from Experts—So Become an Expert

# PART 20
# Grab Bag of Ideas

## Bonus Chapter

# FOREWORD

A few years ago I decided to take one of the greatest risks I have ever taken by starting my first business while I was still pastoring a church in one of the poorest communities in inner-city Detroit. My plan was to create an inflatable games rental business and use it to employ and educate the kind of at-risk young people that I was trying to reach through my church. My wife thought I was crazy.

After wasting a year trying to get the new company established I remember making a call to Jim for some expert marketing advice. Up to that point I had only tried one marketing technique, which was direct mail, and it was costing me an arm and a leg with very limited success.

In one 2-hour phone conversation Jim coached me through and introduced me to several of the methods that you are about to learn. The results were evident quickly. We posted a 200 percent increase in profits over the first 45 days of implementing Jim's strategies. I was quickly able to start hiring many of the type of people I was trying to reach. This was the start of something big.

After the quick success and results I received from Jim's coaching I quickly found numerous local business owners coming to me for advice to help their own businesses grow so they could get the same type of results that I did. I worked with owners of a photography and media business, a professional sound and lighting company, a Bible bookstore, a copy and print shop and several other business owners. The results were astounding! In almost every case where the business followed through on the strategies (the same ones in this book), the businesses grew substantially. Get ready to learn from one of the most creative and proven marketing strategists you will find. Get ready to accomplish the goals and objectives you have set for yourself, your family, and your business, organization, or ideas.

May God bless you in whatever assignment you have in life and may you experience tremendous results in following the wisdom and coaching of one of His finest!

**Pastor Kevin Ramsby**
**HopeVillageDetroit.com**

All proceeds generated from sales of this book will go to support the mission of Hope Village Detroit.

# PREFACE

## ELEVEN OF THE GREAT IDEAS IN THIS BOOK

1. You *must* play defense with Google Alerts.

Six steps to monitoring and managing your online reputation while also spying on what your competitors are up to. See Chapter 2.

2. You *must* set-up a free Facebook page for your business.

Does your business show up in the third-largest country on earth? Put the most powerful social network on earth to work for your business for free. See Chapter 47.

3. You *must* automate your e-mail efforts.

You'll never run a higher-return marketing campaign than e-mail. Here's how to do it right even on a tiny budget. See Chapter 53.

4. You *must* post 24 short and simple videos online. Are you clueless about what videos to put online? These are the questions your customers are asking and they love seeing your video response. See Chapter 37.

5. You *must* make your mark on Google Maps.

You can improve what Google says about your business if you follow these five steps. See Chapter 16.

6. You *must* think viral.

"Going viral" isn't just for funny videos about kids and small pets. Get your message spread fast by tapping into the power of viral video. See Chapter 48.

7. You *must* automate the process you use to supply quality content to prospects and then follow up with them in powerfully creative ways. See Chapter 94.

8. You *must* realize that you'll never again be your own best salesman.

Your fans, partners, and customer testimonials are all far better at selling you and your business than you will ever be—it's time to start leveraging your real sales force! See Chapter 70.

9. You *must* improve your guarantee and return policy.

Unless it feels a little insane when you are done, it's not good enough. See Chapter 3.

10. You *must* accommodate cell phone users.

The entire Internet is being rebuilt for smartphone users. What are you going to do about it? See Part 8.

11. You *must* take the bad name test.

Odds are your website domain name stinks and you don't even know it. Here's a five-minute fix that anyone can afford. No website changes or geek assistance required. See Chapter 20.

# Introduction: Marketing Is Now Free!

I'm not against spending money on marketing; it's just that the most effective strategies available for spreading the word are now free.

Without spending a dime on marketing or advertising, my partner and I established one of my membership websites a couple of years ago that now has about 9,000 members as of this writing. Thousands of members log on weekly and pay us monthly for the right to access the targeted content and training we provide there. I won't tell you the name of the site for now because that's not the point. The point is this site is just one of the several income streams I've established without spending *any* money on marketing.

It's not that I am against spending on marketing; it's just that I've found that all of the most effective strategies available are now free or virtually free.

It's as if marketing and advertising have been *freed* from the clutches of the old, established giants and expensive strategies that use to control them. Even if you stop reading this book right now you'll have learned a great lesson—that marketing is now free—thanks mostly to the Internet.

### More facts of note about this membership site that my partner and I run

- Not only have my partner and I never met, we have never spoken! We've been working together steadily for over three years and have never had the occasion to speak. The discussions that I have with my partner have all happened by e-mail. He lives in Australia and I live in the United States. It's not that we avoid each other; it's a time zone and convenience issue. Finding powerful marketing partners who you can trust has never been easier than it is today, yet few of us are taking advantage of this fact.

- For a few dollars per month we manage an e-mail list of around 14,000 people interested in the niche that our website serves. The loyal followers who make up that list have generated hundreds of thousands of dollars in profits for us as we promote our own products as well as carefully screened awesome products from others that we receive an affiliate commission for. Again—no marketing expenses.
- One of the best sources of new members on our site has been our loyal membership base. We give them an incentive to spread the word by paying them a percentage of the fees collected for each new member they bring us (that's the closest thing we have to a marketing expense). Online we call this type of arrangement *affiliate marketing* and it's a powerful free way to gain exposure for any business. It's purely pay-for-performance marketing. I call it free marketing and it's covered later in this book.
- The income stream from this website is just one of several income streams that I manage, but in all cases my advertising and marketing budgets are zero or virtually zero. My accountant can barely believe the numbers when she sees them. My marketing and advertising budget is peanuts, yet I'm one of her top clients with multiple thriving businesses.

## MY $36,000 STUNT: CALL IT FREE MARKETING ON EBAY!

I ran an auction on eBay with a starting bid of $1 not too long ago. The winning bidder received the opportunity to co-author a book with me and then keep all the money the book ever made. The final bid was over $36,000 and the winning bidder, Stuart Turnbull, said recently that he can hardly describe the positive experience that this has been for him. He's created multiple, automated, marketing-free income streams since that time as well.

The free publicity and new readers and followers that I gained were worth far more than the nice payday I received from the auction.

What were my marketing expenses? The eBay fees that I paid after the auction was over. It was a few hundred dollars.

I'd like to teach you to see marketing the way I see it, if I may.

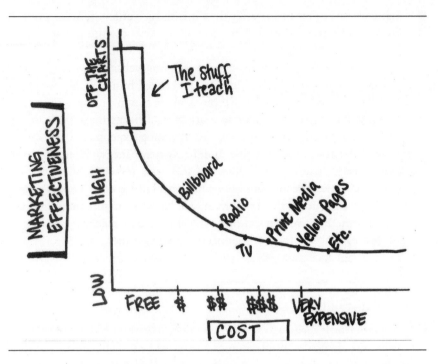

## WHO IS THIS BOOK FOR?

There's a good chance we have something in common. I'm busy, and so are you. Being busy is as common as breathing for those of us trying to change the world (or our part of it), so I'll get right to the point.

If I can have a moment I'll help you make the right decision about whether or not you should take the time to read some or (for the truly committed) all of this book.

**Here are a few questions I'd be asking if I were in your shoes right now:**
1. Will these ideas expand the reach of my ideas or my business?
2. How easy is it for me to implement these ideas?
3. Do I have to read this whole book in order to benefit?
4. Are *all* of the ideas taught in this book *really* free to implement?

If you have a business to grow, a message to share, a mission that needs supporters, a website that needs viewers, an invention, or even a dream that you are trying to share, grow, expand, or launch then this book *is* for you. The goal of this book is to help make those things happen.

## WILL IT WORK FOR YOU?

I believe it will because I have a proven history of helping make these things happen for myself and for others—especially when it comes to creatively using the Internet as an effective and inexpensive (free, in most cases) marketing tool.

Over 100,000 people and businesses have paid me for my marketing and business advice in the form of coaching, books, membership websites, and so on, and something very rewarding typically happens in these exchanges. I don't just teach, but I learn something new each time.

---

### CASE STUDY

After much arm-twisting I finally convinced a real estate client of mine that he should giveaway a training course that he'd spent thousands of dollars and countless hours perfecting. He had only sold a few copies until I convinced him to start giving it all away. Once we did that we started generating tens of thousands of dollars monthly in coaching contracts almost instantly.

---

As a result of all the interesting people and businesses I've worked with I've become a collector of effective marketing ideas. I have used and seen these ideas at work in my own business efforts, as well as in the businesses of my students and clients, and, in many cases, they have achieved amazing results for nearly a decade. None of these businesses are making big marketing or advertising investments at any point along the way. It's still striking to me how freely available this whole new world of massive exposure and marketing really is.

This is not a read it from cover-to-cover book. Not every idea will apply to you, but I hope you'll find that *most* ideas will.

This book is a brainstorm of ideas presented in a way that they can be absorbed easily and quickly implemented. Each idea is very budget friendly, if not entirely free. It's not about saving money as much as it's about effective marketing.

Most of the strategies I'll be sharing revolve around using the Internet as a powerful marketing tool, but there are plenty of non-Internet related strategies as well.

I've broken the book loosely into three major sections. The first 32 chapters will help you get found online and establish or protect your reputation. I discuss what I consider to be the new habits and rules that we all must embrace in order to thrive in an economy built on instant virtual relationships and the limitless free flow of information.

In the middle of the book, from Chapters 33 through 77, I discuss building trust and growing your circle of influence. Your message needs to be informational, attention grabbing, and potent. I also try to drive home the lesson that the most influential and successful people among us are those who are creating the best content for their audience to consume.

Consider Chapter 78 through the end of the book the third section. This section will prepare you for whatever is coming next. These are the foundations that will keep you relevant, interesting, and potent no matter what the future holds. Throughout this book I mention services and websites that offer tools or resources that you might want more information about. I keep a current link to these services and sites on a dedicated resource page located here: 101FreeMarketing.com.

If you stop by that page be sure to register with your e-mail address and I'll send you relevant updates as well as book updates. You can also actively participate in helping update and add to this book by leaving your thoughts and comments. Help me write an even better book by adding your stories and insights! I look forward to hearing from you as you apply these ideas and succeed.

**Jim Cockrum**
**101FreeMarketing.com**

# PART 1

# BUILD YOUR REPUTATION—OR YOUR BRAND—FOR FREE

*Your character is what you really are while your reputation is merely what others think you are.*

—John R. Wooden

I couldn't agree more with this quote from the late great coach Wooden. The reality on the Internet is that very few prospects will ever care to find out who you really are deep inside as an organization, business, or individual.

The busy, overwhelmed public will make snap decisions based on a quick glance at your online reputation.

Whether your online reputation or brand is accurate or not matters very little to the masses. Which is why you can't afford to ignore it by thinking that it's entirely based on your good character, or the handful of testimonials on your own website.

Monitoring and managing your online reputation has recently become just as vital as any other marketing you may be doing. It's time to play defense.

The term *reputation management* may be new to you, but it's a term that you must embrace because of the new rules of the Internet economy. Under the old rules if you upset a customer we were all told to expect that they would tell seven of their friends. The implied conclusion was that an occasional upset customer was acceptable and expected, but certainly not potentially devastating.

Now things have changed. If someone has something bad to say about you, their comment could be posted semi-permanently on page one of Google for months or years. This seemingly insignificant act on the part of one customer could potentially impact you negatively in front of hundreds or even thousands of prospects. The fact is, people are increasingly using search engines to research the industries, people, or businesses they are considering doing business with and, like it or not, your business, name, or organization is on the list of those that *will* be impacted. And it gets worse before it gets better, because on Google bad news floats.

The stakes are high. All it takes is one angry customer, one disgruntled employee, or one bad business partner acting on your behalf and your reputation could take a semipermanent hit. Maybe it already has and you don't even know it.

## TOUGH REALITY

A public that rarely takes time to investigate the background of the news reporters they listen to isn't likely to devote any time to researching the motives of the random strangers they encounter online who have something negative to say about you or your company. They'll just believe the negative and move on.

But there is good news. Take a deep breath.

You *can* proactively manage your online reputation whether you are a small local business or a big player with customers worldwide. You don't have to be perfect either—which is good news since none of us are.

In my online businesses I've sold services, products, and downloadable goods to well over 100,000 customers in the past few years with my name and business name proudly attached to every transaction. The price points have ranged from $7 special reports to tens of thousands of dollars for multiyear coaching or consulting contracts. In other words, my own business has been a good testing ground for my theories of reputation management.

The big question: Is it possible to keep 100,000 people 100 percent happy on that many various transactions? The answer is no—that's impossible. No person or organization is perfect.

The realistic goal for your business should be to fix every problem fast, and allow no one to become so upset that they post glaringly negative things about you online. On the occasion where a situation gets away from you, you need to be prepared to combat the negative comment strategically. It is possible to manage your reputation through a large numbers of transactions and customers even if you have only a tiny staff like I do.

The other component of a good strategy involves intentionally flooding the Internet with the good news and testimonials about you and your company to help drown out the inevitable bad news. You'll need the help of loyal customers to do this part correctly (and of course 100 percent ethically).

So, how's my online reputation doing with the odds stacked against me?

One popular watchdog site that monitors those of us claiming to teach Internet business has over 40,000 voting members and ranks over 2,000 industry experts. At the time of this writing I'm thrilled to be consistently ranked in the top five most trusted and have spent a lot of time at number one. Also, the first several pages of Google and other major search engines are filled with positive comments and feedback about me, my websites, and my businesses. It's all because of what I'm about to show you in the next six chapters—my six rules for maintaining a good online reputation. I believe these rules will serve any business very well.

# CHAPTER 1

# SUPERCHARGE YOUR ONLINE REPUTATION

If you read books the way I do, you may be starting out by jumping over the intro and other stuff by going right to Chapter 1. That's a *big* mistake. You really need to check out the Introduction in order to get what I'm saying.

*Virtually every customer has a megaphone and an audience—give them a reason to say great things about you.*

This era of instant online relationships and limitless information is the best time in the history of business to run an honest business that also wows your customers. Customers today have the ability to spread the word to unimaginable numbers of potential prospects if you'll just give them a good reason to. In my business I teach anyone who works for me the power of testimonials and feedback with this simple philosophy, "Any positive comment sent to us or posted online is worth $1,000 in our pocket. No amount of marketing or advertising that you will ever do can compare to the viral power of your audience as they share their experiences and impressions of your business online."

The network of potential contacts that your customers are all a part of is unlike anything we've ever seen in business, and it's growing at an unimaginable pace. If Facebook were a country it would be the third largest country on earth, and it's still growing rapidly as I write this book. You simply must find creative ways to tap into the pool of prospects that are directly connected to your current customers.

Even if you don't have a website. . . .

It's no longer good enough just to be good at what you do. In order to supercharge your online reputation you must proactively encourage your customers to spread the word. You must lead and encourage them instead of waiting on good things to happen on their own. You need the help of your most loyal fans and customers in order to flood the web with good news that will counter and drown out the inevitable bad review that will eventually show up—if it hasn't already. While you can't put words in the mouths of your customers, you can give them every opportunity to say great things about you, and you can encourage them to do so.

Make it easy for your customers to leave feedback online both in front of their online network of friends and contacts, and on review sites. A few examples of this in action:

- Have an Internet-connected laptop or iPad on hand in your business lobby or waiting room and post a sign nearby that reads, "Free Internet access. All we ask in return is that you tell your friends about your experience with us today on Facebook, Twitter, or e-mail us your story at this e-mail address: MyStory@YourBusinessEmail.com."
- Post a sign in your business targeted at customers with smartphones, requesting that they leave a review or post a comment on your blog, website, a popular review site, Twitter, Facebook, and so on while they wait. This little prompt could start a viral wave of activity from just one customer participating.
- In every e-mail or correspondence you send your customers encourage them to send you stories of success or mention your services to their online network of friends. If you give instructions on exactly how to help you it will be very well received by your most loyal customers.
- Most cell phones now have built in powerful cameras, and as a result pictures have become nearly as easy to share as the spoken word. We all know that a good picture is better than a thousand words right? Encourage your customers to use their cell phones to take and send you pictures of their experiences with your business, employees, and products. Encourage them to post them online in their social networks and on review sites (be specific as to which sites).
- Hold contests that encourage your customers to create a simple YouTube.com video talking about you and your business. Reward the most creative entries with a prize. I did this activity with my mailing list of top customers about a year ago and created a great viral wave of new activity and publicity on YouTube.
- Create a high quality T-shirt or other branded items that reflect the marketing message of your business and give them away to top

customers and sell them to others, but take it a step further. Request that customers send you a picture and post a picture of themselves wearing or using the items somewhere online. These photos make for great eye-candy for any website as well if customers send you a copy! If your customers aren't local, use a service like Cafepress.com to manage the printing and shipment of your T-shirts.

## CAUTION

Most of the legitimate feedback and review sites online now use IP tracking to help prevent abuse. This means they can tell if one computer is being used to pad the stats for or against a business. More tips and rules for staying legit are posted at the end of this chapter.

Once we've pulled in positive feedback or testimonials, we post them to our own website where the public can see them almost instantly. We also ask anyone who sends us a great testimonial to please jump on the appropriate feedback sites and leave their comments there. We make it easy for them by providing a link and instructions.

Feedback and reviews posted online from a third party that lacks an agenda will be trusted far more than if you post anything positive about yourself. Honest feedback and conversations left on neutral territory, such as a trusted review site, are worth their weight in gold for your business.

Alternately, it's just as easy to use the Internet to tell the world how rotten you are. Online, bad news floats. This means that if 1,000 people love you and one doesn't like you, the comment from the one angry guy will probably find its way to the top. It's not a kind truth, but it's a truth nonetheless. This truth will guide many of the other rules I show you in the five following sections.

You will have customers post bad things about you online eventually. You need to prepare for this reality. Nothing quenches the pain of a complaint posted online like a host of happy testimonials standing nearby overwhelming the lone complainer. These testimonials and happy stories won't come in on their own, though, and it takes time and great service to get them. You have to go after these stories and testimonials and encourage your customers to give you feedback. People are busy, but if you remind them they are glad to help you out (assuming they like you). As you collect stories of success and gratitude you can post these testimonials on your website, blog, or other sites. You can also encourage your customers to post their comments themselves on popular review sites for your industry, and on their social networks like Facebook and Twitter.

**A few things to keep in mind when gathering and encouraging testimonials:**

- While you can ask for testimonials, don't give customers prizes for submitting them. They must be sincere or you'll risk damaging your credibility.
- Let customers know the specific review websites and services where you'd appreciate their feedback appearing. Register with all possible sites associated with your industry. Here's a partial list to get you started: Yelp.com, Google Places, Bing Local, CitySearch.com, Yahoo! Local, Local.com, MerchantCircle.com, and AngiesList.com.
- Adding testimonials to your own website is some of the best content you can possibly have. It's called *social proof* and it's far more powerful than anything you can ever say about yourself on your site.
- Be aware of FTC rules for posting testimonials. More info can be found at www.FTC.org (search for the most current documents on "Endorsements and Testimonials"). Always be cautious when making specific claims of results—those are murky waters with the FTC.
- Whenever possible post a picture, a name, and a city with any testimonials you put online or in your marketing materials. This increases the credibility factor significantly.
- Never give yourself reviews, let your customers do it.
- Don't encourage customers to submit reviews from a single permanently located computer sitting in your office because the IP address will be identical on all testimonials and this will raise red flags with most legitimate online review sites. Instead encourage the use of smartphones for in-house customer testimonial submissions. For example, a restaurant could post a sign where customers can see it that says: "If we didn't earn a 5-star review on Yelp.com today, please let us know how we can earn it before you leave. We rely heavily on your feedback and reviews."
- Use a service like freeconferencecall.com or any other similar service to capture testimonials. Whenever an excited customer contacts you with a great story to tell, request that they "hold that thought" and then give them your dial-in number for your conference call line. Record the call with the two of you talking, and then edit it to their liking if necessary. I provide more details in the chapter on teleseminars, but you can check out a great example of where I used this very idea myself

recently to capture a conversation I had with an excited student (end of Chapter 30). There are also services that will allow you to capture single dial-in customers and record their testimonial, but I prefer to interact so that it feels more like content.

- Watch for positive posts on your blog and get permission to post the comments in other places.
- Any positive e-mails you get can be used the same way.
- Twitter, Facebook, and any other social media site can be a source of new comments and stories that should be shared with larger audiences as a testimonial.
- Use Google Alerts as mentioned earlier in the book to keep an eye out for good news being shared about you and your business.

## CREATIVE IDEA

Houlihan's restaurant offers (by invitation only) their best customers to join their "HQ" program at www.houlihans.com. Once inside, members get invitations to tastings and are encouraged to then re-port their feedback on review sites like Yelp.com or on their own Facebook.com pages.

# CHAPTER 2

# DEFEND YOUR REPUTATION WITH SIMPLE FREE TOOLS

*Monitor the entire Internet for any information that could influence your reputation.*

**D**id you know that you can get automatic daily (or even up to the minute) notification showing you exactly where your name, product, business name, or industry is being discussed online?

There's really only one tool you'll need in order to put a very good monitoring plan in place, and it's free. While there are paid services available that can help you monitor your reputation, I've never used or needed anything except the free options.

I use free Google Alerts to notify me whenever any new content or discussions pop up online that contain the keywords I'm tracking. Once you set up the alerts you'll get an e-mail each time any new content or comments appear on any open access website that is monitored by Google (which is pretty much all of them). You can set the alerts to be sent to you immediately, daily, or weekly depending on your preferences.

To set up your free Google Alerts for your relevant search terms visit this site: www.Google.com/alerts.

**Here are some creative ways to use alerts to defend yourself:**
- Set up alerts for your business name, the names of all key leaders in your business, and any keyword terms relevant to your industry. It's not unusual to have many alerts set up.

10

- Set up alerts for your website domain names to see when and how they are mentioned.
- Monitor the web for plagiarism of your material. To do this set an alert for a particularly unique sentence or phrase from any content you publish online.
- Monitor the activity of any disgruntled reporters, customers, or employees (by name) who you suspect might post something negative online. The earlier you can catch a negative post about you the better able you'll be to defend against it.
- Take these same steps with Twitter using TweetBeep.com.

Toward the end of the book I also show you some ways to play offense (as opposed to just defense) with Google Alerts.

It's important in this chapter to point out that in many businesses (especially in small businesses) the personal reputation of the owner is steadily becoming more and more tied to the reputation of the business they own and vice versa. You must be prepared to proactively protect both reputations because they are so easily linked. The trend of linking business with personal is an unavoidable virtual marriage that you may not even realize is happening, but in the minds of your customers it's likely already happened.

> Several companies are emerging that are set up to help you defend your online reputation. Two such companies are ReputationDefender.com and Naymz.com. Most people haven't embraced the idea of paying someone to help them monitor and manage their online reputation, but the millions of users of the free version of Naymz is just another sign to me that this is a serious emerging trend.

Even for large corporations we are more interested than ever as consumers in the reputations of those running the businesses that we do business with. The research required to investigate businesses and those who run them is becoming very simple; many prospects engage in some online detective work before deciding who they will do business with. You've been warned—no matter how big you are.

Make sure you have a system in place to monitor the web for those who are saying both good and bad things about you and your business.

# CHAPTER 3

# Turn Bad Reviews into Free Marketing

**In this chapter I cover:**
- How to turn negative customer experiences into positives for your business.
- Why and when you should encourage customers to complain.
- How I've implemented these ideas myself with success.

## Turn Negative Customer Experiences into Positives

Complaints happen. It's inevitable that one will be posted online about you or your business.

The good news is that an online customer complaint can often be turned into a positive if caught quickly and dealt with in a friendly, accommodating way.

You not only need a plan in place to monitor the web for comments about you and your business (as discussed in Chapter 2), but you also need to be prepared to respond quickly and professionally to any negative comments. Make sure someone is assigned the task of monitoring the web for comments left about you and your business and also task them with responding appropriately.

Ideally you have several loyal customers who are also willing and ready to come to your defense when the occasion arises. If you run a solid business and have close contact with top customers it's a reasonable request to point out an unfair negative comment to your loyal fans and ask that they respond by leaving honest feedback on top of the offending comment.

Nothing defuses a negative remark like a gang of loyal customers following up in the same forum with several positive remarks specifically addressing the concerns of the unsatisfied customer.

Oftentimes you can win over an unhappy customer with a heartfelt gesture from the top leadership of your business. You can defuse the high emotions of a disgruntled customer nearly every time with a direct phone call or gesture from the top brass in your company. Once the customer is made happy you can request that they modify or remove the negative comment that they left online. Be careful that this isn't done in such a way that it feels like a bribe. Approach the situation as if you are rectifying a wrong, and then let them know how important your online reputation is to your business. Ask them to help you preserve your nearly perfect record. I've found that the vast majority of people respond very well to this and like being asked to help.

Often negative feedback left on review sites can't be altered or deleted, but at a minimum you can try to make sure that a positive comment from the same customer or alternately from other different customers appears nearby any negative comment. If you are able to "make it right" when a customer complains, and you can get them to post a follow-up message on top of their complaint, then virtually no damage has been done and you've likely even earned additional credibility with future prospects who see the online exchange in the coming weeks, months, or even years.

## REAL LIFE EXAMPLE

A customer of mine was upset and he went straight to a popular discussion chat forum to tell the world what we had done wrong before we had any notice from him or a chance to fix it.

Fortunately I saw the forum post and personally responded and soothed things over a bit. After that, several of my top customers also chimed in (without my prompting) and a bit of a debate ensued with the customer, but in the end all was well and I forgot about it.

I had no idea at the time how important that short online forum discussion would become for my business over the next several years because something surprising happened next.

That simple forum discussion suddenly appeared on top of Google and remained on page one for four years because several of the top keywords related to my business showed up in that discussion. Even after the discussion forum website was no longer available for new members, and even after the discussion forum was no longer even being used by anyone, the same page kept showing up on page one of

Google. A short online forum discussion that had occurred over the course of a few days nearly four years earlier had an impact on my business for several years. That one forum thread was read by thousands of prospects and was part of their initial experience and impression of my company and me. I knew this was true, because several prospects would mention that they'd seen it. You need to have a plan for dealing with this type of unpredictable situation.

## Encourage Customer Complaints *before* They Have a Chance to Go Public

The best strategy to contain negative comments (besides offering great service, of course) is to give your customers a controlled forum in which to vent before they have a chance to go public. At any point where your customer might have feedback to give, make sure you are there nearby with a suggested strategy for accepting their feedback and complaints. Consider going so far as to literally invite complaints so that you can control and respond and diffuse them before they get out into the uncontrollable public forum online.

---

### EXAMPLE

Einstein Bros. (the bagel company) maintains an active Facebook page where customers can instantly leave feedback including complaints and know that company representatives are paying attention and responding to concerns. In this way they can effectively contain the spread of bad news while giving their customers a forum in which to vent concerns.

---

*Here Are Some Ways I've Used This Strategy in Some of My Online Businesses* In my eBay business we've shipped thousands of products all over the world without a single negative comment from any customers. A 10-year perfect feedback score on eBay is a rare thing.

Does this mean there has never been a complaint? Of course not! We are simply proactive about capturing customer complaints before they go public. Being proactive means that we give all customers an easily accessed hot line they can use to complain at any point in the transaction process. For example, we ship each item with a prominently placed note inside the package telling our customer that we fully expect to receive perfect 5-star

feedback. If they aren't prepared to give us great feedback, then we request that they contact us so we can earn it.

After we earn 5-star feedback we then request their feedback.

By doing this, I've done business for 10 years on eBay without one negative customer feedback mark on my primary eBay account.

Another example:

Whenever my outbound call center team calls on interested prospects, I *refuse* to allow them to use any pressure sales strategies (this goes against the industry trend in a big way). Instead, we use an effective "leave them better than you found them" policy that works as simply as it sounds. We always offer prospects that say "yes" or "no" a free service or product of significant value in exchange for their time. We do this because time is valuable and we don't want to steal any from prospects. This is not only the right thing to do, but it is a proactive way of preventing complaints. Also, we never allow the phone call to end badly. If that means I have to send a letter to them personally, I'll do it. The telephone is a powerful marketing tool, but if used incorrectly you can quickly generate complaints online for your business. We prevent that with multiple strategies for handling customers with the utmost care and respect.

Complaints will always happen, but your ability to capture and deal with them will go a long way towards protecting your online reputation. Be prepared to go so far as to invite complaints and keep them inside a controlled environment in order to protect what is said about you in public forums online.

| Who in your business is assigned the task of monitoring and responding to any threats against your brand?

# CHAPTER 4

# USE YOUR EXPERT KNOWLEDGE TO CREATE CUSTOMER-ATTRACTING CONTENT

*Your business's reputation is not only dependent on the quality of your products and services, but also on the quality of the content that you are able to create and freely distribute online. No matter what your product or service is, you must start creating informative, educational, or entertaining content.*

Throughout this book I address in greater detail both the importance of creating content and various ways to go about doing it in simple and free or virtually free ways.

Behind every purchase is a decision. Behind every decision is information. He who has the best information distributed in the most creative ways *wins*.

You might be asking why I have included a chapter about content creation in the section of the book that's supposed to be about online reputation. I'm including it here because your reputation is determined by a new level of expectations that your prospects have.

**Your prospects want:**
- More from you with less effort on their part.
- Someone to educate them on the best decisions possible, without any selfish motivations, even if it means sending them to a competitor at times.

- To know that they are working with an expert, as evidenced by a large following of consumers eagerly taking in your content.
- To feel like they have a degree of influence over the content and services they have available to them. They want interaction with you.
- The right information at the right time handed to them.

Even traditional retail-types of businesses are starting to recognize this trend. Visit the website PGeverydaySolutions.com to see how a nearly $80 billion company is starting to apply the principle of educating consumers via content creation even in the retail off-the-shelf market.

> The winning businesses will be the businesses that are best able to create quality content that assists customers online in making wise choices...even if the advice and content points your prospects away from doing business with you and toward a better solution for them.

**Here are some ideas that will help you formulate a plan for putting quality content into the hands of prospects who are online right now:**

- Make a list of the most commonly asked questions that you get from your prospects. If you aren't sure what these questions are, then conduct a survey among your best customers. Another great source of ideas is your customer support e-mail archives, as well as your top salesmen if you use them.
- Make a list of the questions that your prospects *should* be asking.
- Describe your ideal customer as specifically as possible.
- Make a list of the problems that your products solve.
- Make a list of the benefits that your products give.

This *is not* an exercise in listing out the features of your products. This is about identifying the questions that your ideal prospects might be asking while they are in the research phase of their buying journey.

Once you have completed this exercise you will have a framework for creating quality content that will appeal to your target market. This content can take various forms, but some options are blog posts, video, or audio recordings such as podcasts, special reports, and so on.

Your content should directly address the questions that are being asked by your prospects. For example, a report might be titled "Ten Things Every First Time Home Buyer Should Know About Insurance."

Besides the obvious benefits of educating your prospects towards a purchasing decision, there are also other not so obvious benefits to producing quality content for free public consumption online. Here are some examples.

## BECOME A CELEBRITY IN YOUR NICHE

Radio hosts, TV producers, and news writers are continually on the lookout for experts in any number of niche markets. Having your name and your business's name associated with generous amounts of quality content online can only lead to good things and free publicity even off of the Internet. For example, I am frequently contacted by radio shows, magazines, and newspaper reporters requesting my opinions on various topics related to running a business online. These requests for my assistance are all generated as a result of the free content I've distributed online regarding this topic.

## FIND GREAT PARTNERS

Creative partnerships are formed online all the time. The businesses and experts who are best able to get their name out there will also be the ones who are contacted by the most creative potential partners. For example, I told you at the beginning of this book about my partner Andrew who I found while doing some simple Internet research for a business idea I had. The two of us went on to establish what has since grown into a thriving 9,000-member membership website. The beauty of this example is the fact that I live in the United States and he lives in Australia so our business hours are very different. After knowing each other for three years we have never even spoken on the phone. The entire business has been built by e-mail. None of this would've happened had my partner not been willing to create and freely distribute quality content that built and confirmed his expertise in my target niche.

## GET FOUND ON THE SEARCH ENGINES

Creating and distributing quality content online will increase your exposure on search engines and will lead to increased traffic and exposure for your business or websites. You'll also get valuable links from other websites to your site that will continually improve your search engine rank.

Having a free content distribution strategy is discussed in more detail in Part 11 of this book.

# CHAPTER 5

# INSANE REFUND POLICY PROFITS

*Give speedy refunds to those who request them. Refunds are no longer only for those who deserve them, but for* anyone *who requests them, and often even for undeserving customers.*

**P**erhaps the greatest secret to my success in guarding my reputation has been to give quick refunds to anyone who asks for one, no matter how irrational or irresponsible the customer's request is. This is the case even when I'm going to lose a lot of money to an unrealistic or rude, undeserving customer.

No matter how expensive the refund is to me, the cost pales in comparison to having comments from an angry, ranting customer show up on page one of any search engine when a search is performed on my name or for the name of my business.

Bottom line: A generous refund policy is vital if you are to avoid getting negative feedback left against you online.

Here's how extreme this policy can be:

One high-volume eBay seller I coached sold expensive collectible items. These were all one-of-a-kind items that weren't easy to replace if they were broken or damaged in transit. The items were also difficult to describe perfectly to his buyers, so post-purchase disputes occasionally arose. He was having trouble haggling back and forth with customers who wanted full or partial refunds on items, and his eBay feedback score (reputation score) and website reputation were taking a hit as a result of what he called unreasonable customers.

I advised him to implement the most generous imaginable refund and return policy he could stomach, and then make it hurt even worse by cranking it up a notch, and then get back to me with the results a few months later.

The policy I suggested went something like this: "The buyer of this item may return the item at any point for a full refund of all expenses paid with no questions asked. We will issue the full refund *before* you ship the item back so that you aren't nervous about your money being kept. We will pay the return shipping, and even if the item is damaged on its way back to us, we'll take the hit. If you aren't happy you don't pay and you'll never have to wait for your refund. It's that simple."

Sounds insane right?

It's not crazy; it's just an attempt to play by the new rules where customers have all the control.

Here's what happened:

After implementing my suggested aggressive refund policy, his sales sky-rocketed, his profits improved, and his reputation was perfect since I last checked in on him. He took my advice and on only a few occasions was he asked to issue a refund before the return item was shipped to him. Most people just don't expect that even if you offer it.

Not one theft had occurred (yet), but he indicated that even if an occasional theft or shipping damage incident did occur, that he'd gladly take the hit and move on because his bidding action and sales rates were so much higher than they were before.

The cost of not taking my advice would have lead to damaging negative comments and less business overall. The cost of just one negative comment left anywhere online can be astronomical and it must be avoided.

While this type of refund policy isn't possible in all cases (for example, a custom home builder probably can't offer this), the heart of the idea is to do everything possible to avoid negative remarks online.

While we are on the topic of being irrational, I have several more challenging ideas for you in Chapter 6.

# CHAPTER 6

# BEING IRRATIONAL IS GREAT MARKETING

*You can't afford to offer anything less than irrationally generous, loyalty-building services and products. Remember: Each customer has a megaphone, so give them something over the top to shout about to their hundreds or thousands of listening friends.*

The positive impact of being irrationally generous has never been more evident than it is now. It clearly pays to have a highly ethical and customer-centered business approach. The benefits are so obvious that even the most expensive customer-centered policies and activities, that used to be too far above and beyond expectations, are now on the table as a fantastic investment that will almost certainly and quickly pay you back.

> You've been warned: The customer service activities that were previously considered irrationally overboard and were reserved for only top customers are now vital to your survival and success. That same service level should be used on all customers and it will pay off handsomely.

If you don't believe that the irrational customer service approach can be applied to any business then go do some research on the customer service habits of zappos.com (an online shoe seller) and you'll quickly see my point. Among their irrational policies is a 365-day return policy on any shoes. That's nuts, but it's working because of the viral power of their fan base that raves loyally and consistently online to an ever-growing network of contacts. When a zappos.com fan experiences poor customer service

21

from any other business their mantra is, "Why can't that business just be more like Zappos?"

In Chapter 3 I made a case for actually encouraging your customers to complain, and in Chapter 5 I tried to convince you that more refunds can actually be better for your business than fewer refunds. If you thought those ideas were a little irrational, then I have several more irrational habits for you to consider. Before I'm done you'll either be convinced or you'll think I'm crazy!

The following irrational strategies work well because of the immediate impact these over-the-top gestures have on your customers and their highly attentive networks of connections.

Five Irrational Habits That Supercharge Your Online Reputation.

## Irrational Habit 1: Don't Keep Secrets; Expose Them!

What do magic tricks, restaurant recipes, and video game cheat codes all have in common?

The answer, of course, is that the mystery is over. It's all out there online, and in each case many people got rich and grew a nice circle of loyal followers by exposing this secret information to the masses.

Have you noticed that it's getting harder and harder for any business to keep a secret?

Consider the irrational step of exposing your business or industry secrets before someone else does. If there is enough interest in the topic, you could create a flood of loyalty and influence among a new customer base that would otherwise have been impossible to reach. You'll also have the opportunity to operate in a business model that enjoys the highest possible profit margin in the history of business—selling information!

In the world of limitless information there are very few secrets that are safe for the long term. If you don't expose a valuable secret now, someone else probably will eventually, and in doing so they will win the influence and trust of the audience that is eager to learn the truth.

A personal example:

One of the first products that I sold online over 10 years ago was event tickets. I got very good at securing good seats for highly-sought-after events from the major ticket sellers online.

I taught myself the rules of eBay regarding event tickets, and I studied all applicable laws for the ticket brokering industry. I spent many Saturday mornings anxiously applying my creative strategies so that I could secure tickets in the first few rows of major events scheduled all over the United States. I would then sell these tickets to the highest bidders on eBay, making up to a 1,000 percent profit in some cases.

As my business grew, my profits plateaued at about $800 to $1,000 dollars per week as I worked a few hours most weekends. I already had a steady full-time job and I didn't want to run this as a full-time business. I settled into a one-year comfort zone, but something uncomfortable started happening. I started noticing more and more competitors on eBay.

A large number of my ticket-buying customers were inquiring with me about how I so consistently was able to acquire such great seats at such popular events. It seemed that many of them were starting to figure out some of my secrets. I was at a decision point. Had I made the incorrect choice at that moment it would have cost me millions of dollars over the next decade.

The choice I had in front of me was to keep my secrets to myself and continue earning some decent side income while working against an ever-growing pool of competitors, or I could expose the secrets that only a handful of studious eBay and online ticket sellers were privileged to, and possibly get out of the business I was in while helping others start up a nice side income online.

The choice I made is obvious, isn't it? I exposed my secrets to the world.

At that point I wrote a simple 20-page document exposing all that I knew about how to secure great tickets for concerts and sporting events. Needless to say, many of my eBay competitors were quite unhappy with me at the time. At first I gave this report away for free to any customer who spent a significant dollar amount on my tickets. It was a nice bonus for them. Many of those first customers who bought tickets from me on eBay over a decade ago are still some of my most loyal followers as I continue down the path of teaching others the secrets of running profitable businesses on the Internet.

That same report went on to bring in tens of thousands of dollars as a $20 downloadable report. Within just a few weeks of writing that report I got into the business of creating content online and left the business of selling event tickets far behind. Since that time I've sold tens of thousands of copies of various reports, books, and courses all in the arena of Internet marketing and Internet business. I've launched two membership websites with a combined membership of over 10,000, and I've been doing all of this full time since 2002.

It all started with exposing a secret.

Would you giveaway a secret that was earning you $1,000 per day in profits *knowing* that by exposing your secret your income from the idea would be eliminated?

If you are smart you would!

Jeremy Schoemaker did just that a few years ago and it was a great business decision. Jeremy (affectionately known as "ShoeMoney" online) famously gave away the exact details of his online marketing campaign that was earning him about $1,000 per day in profit. I met him in person at an affiliate marketing conference where he gave me permission to share his story. Jeremy bravely (or irrationally, if you prefer) decided to publicly expose his entire business model online, knowing that he was effectively killing his niche secret because he was sure to be copied by so many others almost instantly. The good news, though, is that as a result of his irrational generosity with his secrets he quickly grew a massive, loyal audience of thousands who now enjoy his affiliate marketing blog. The income from his popular blog now earns him far more money than he'd ever have earned by keeping his secrets to himself.

Here's another example, from a doll-clothing seller who got creative by giving away her secrets.

We started Liberty Jane Clothing on eBay a couple of years ago. My wife was truly great at making 18-inch doll clothes, so we quickly found a following. Twelve months later we were PowerSellers, and making around $1,000 per month. One month we excitedly topped $1,500. The problem was that we had reached the limit of our business model (which consisted of sewing outfits one at a time and listing them on eBay one at a time). Although we were happy to be making some nice side money, she was burned out, so we really needed to figure out a new approach.

Unfortunately our operation just wasn't sustainable, or scalable. We needed to figure out how to leverage her unique skill, while freeing up her time. We had already decided that making mass-manufactured items, or selling other peoples' mass-manufactured items, wasn't right for us. Hiring people didn't seem right for us either. We felt stuck.

Then we got your book *The Silent Sales Machine*. The message was clear—build an e-mail list, and offer digital products to your customers.

The entire next summer we debated publishing my wife's patterns as PDF guidebooks. We knew we could do it, but worried about whether it was the right business strategy. It felt like a huge gamble. We worried about creating an army of competitors who would use her patterns to undermine her auction prices, as well as if other people would take her work and go further than we'd been able to up to that point. Finally that fall we decided to trust Jim's advice and go digital.

That month we set up a new site, www.libertyjanepatterns.com, published a few patterns as PDF guidebooks, offered some for free, and ended the month having sold 11. It was the start of a new product category for us that had one huge benefit: it was easily scalable.

Within six months our pattern guidebooks category was making as much as our eBay auctions ever had, and the decision to offer digital products proved to be a no-brainer. None of our fears materialized, and we've discovered more benefits than we could have imagined. Today we are adding over 100 people per week to our newsletter list, and last month we had over 2,200 patterns downloaded. We have over 2,500 YouTube subscribers, and over 2,600 Facebook fans. Our business model today includes multiple digital products, downloads, and coaching courses. By allowing other seamstresses to use our patterns for sew-from-home businesses for free (we call them partners), we've actually created an interesting secondary market that hasn't diminished the value of our original outfits—instead it enhanced them. In the near future we are working to overhaul our websites to accommodate the continued growth, and we're working on publishing two exciting new books that we know will be a hit with our customers.

Thanks for publishing *The Silent Sales Machine*, Jim!

### Irrational Habit 2: Eagerly Send Customers to a Competitor If It's Best for Them

Have you ever been in a store and asked for help finding a particular item, but the worker was unable to provide you what you needed? In some rare cases when this happens the worker will lean in real close and in a low whisper mention the name of the nearby competitor who can help you with what you need. The employee is nervous about being caught and punished for doing the right thing.

Don't let that happen to your business on or offline. Not only is it bad business, but this type of protective attitude will rob you of the influence and loyalty not only of your customers, but of the potential exposure you could have to their networks of contacts as they brag about how open you are about helping your customers.

Be good at what you are good at, and refer your customers to the "best of the best" when it's not you.

Not only should you not hesitate to refer your customers to capable competitors, you should instead jump at the chance to do so whenever it makes the most sense for your customers.

These are just the type of noteworthy experiences that socially connected customers will want to share online, and it will be your business that they are bragging about.

## Irrational Habit 3: Sell Only to Your Mom

It should go without saying that you have a responsibility to provide excellent products and services. Irrational habit number three goes a step well beyond this though, because now I'm challenging you to be authentic with your marketing and advertising activities as well.

Your prospects are becoming increasingly irritated by self-serving, sales-pitch-sounding messages. The litmus test I use when writing advertising copy is quite simple and it has worked for me very well for several years. My guiding principle is to sell only to a friend or to my mom when writing copy. Talk to that one person and treat them like you'd treat a true friend.

If you find yourself using language that you would never use in a dinner conversation with family and friends, then you are probably violating this principle and your reputation will likely suffer. Nobody likes to be sold to, but everyone enjoys discussing good ideas and interesting products with family and friends.

> As one of my long-time students and readers, Julie Anna Schultz began growing an e-mail list of her own.
>
> Recently she wrote to tell me that one of the most valuable lessons I'd taught her was this very lesson:
>
> "I began to care deeply about the people on my list with the common ground of what I loved to do. A "Jimism" that has made the most money for me is to write as if I am talking to only one person, not a group of people.
>
> That one person ideally is my mom—that's who I keep in mind while I am recommending products or writing about my passion. If I'm not comfortable recommending or talking shop the way I do to my mom, I need to rethink my strategy."
>
> Julie enjoys her large family of 11 while running an active online business from home. With three of her oldest kids helping, she sells books online, runs a consulting membership website, offers training materials, does affiliate marketing, and even conducts live seminars.

## Irrational Habit 4: Give Stuff Away

One of the best ways to ignite a viral whirlwind of activity about you and your products is to giveaway something that your better judgment tells you should be sold. The higher the real and perceived value of this product the better your end results will be. Some of my favorite giveaway products are high quality, relevant information products (a training course, a book, a video product, etc.). Information costs little to deliver but can have a very high perceived and actual value for those that receive it. I'm not talking about a sales pitch product here. I'm talking about valuable information that establishes your credibility and delivers very high value, just-in-time information to the customer.

This principle is best illustrated with a true story from one of my recent clients. The lesson behind the story applies to virtually any business model.

A real estate client of mine had a very successful approach to selling houses using Internet leads that he'd been generating himself. Because of his high sales volume he was setting records and getting the attention of nearly every agency in his large local market. He sought my advice on how to best market his unusual process to other realtors.

I told him we needed to capture his story as well as his process in a training course, and that's what we set about doing.

We spent several months thoroughly documenting the process that he'd been using. Once the process had been put into a course format, my client was quite proud of what we had created. The course we had built literally spelled out step-by-step every detail of the process used to sell homes at a fast clip using self-generated Internet leads. It truly was worth thousands of dollars in the hands of the right person.

Then I dropped an irrational bombshell on him. I told him it was time to give it all away.

He balked.

In fairness, I hadn't told him that I intended to giveaway the course for free until *after* we'd finished it. I didn't want him thinking that we were building a freebie course that would potentially lack the depth and value of a paid course. He fully intended to sell the course all along and thought that this would be his new income stream, but I had a larger vision for it.

My advice was to giveaway the highly valuable, very thorough product that we had created and use it to generate leads and build his credibility for a high-end "we do it for you" service and coaching program for overly busy, ineffective real estate agents. My theory was that it wouldn't be hard to get names, e-mail addresses, and phone numbers from prospects in exchange for a course worth thousands of dollars. The obvious risk, of course, was that agents would simply take the course for free and use it themselves without ever contacting us and without ever buying anything from us, but I knew that meant they would have to work, study, learn, and apply what we were showing them, and most people aren't willing or able to do that! They'd rather write a check.

At this point my client had a decision to make. He wanted to sell our course and I wanted to give it away. The decision was his, and he chose to have me help him sell the course against my better judgment.

Giving it all away wasn't a risk he was willing to take, yet.

He sold several copies of the course online and made a few thousand dollars. But it wasn't worth the effort for all the work we'd done. We just couldn't get it ramped up in the crowded real estate education market. We had to do a lot of convincing just to make the sale, and he got turned down a lot.

Next we tried it my way.

Almost instantly the fully downloadable course began spreading across the Internet like wildfire. Thousands reviewed the course and were exposed to my client's brilliant creativity, and in many cases they sought him out for advice and coaching. He was quickly established as a credible expert on par with even the most sought-after real estate gurus. The beauty of being an expert is that you can charge more money for your time. Once we knew what the typical needs were of those who had taken the course, we set up a high-end coaching and "do it for you" offer based on customer feedback. We quickly had hundreds of clients and were billing tens of thousands of dollars monthly on autopilot. Of course he was also getting great results for his clients.

The lesson? Create amazing information and then *give it away.*

There are other great stories in this book about the power of giving stuff away in Chapters 34, 43, and other places as well.

Other sections of this book cover the topics of creating and distributing high-quality content, but keep in mind that giving great content away for free is nearly always a great lead generation strategy, especially when the product you are giving away has a high perceived value.


## Irrational Habit 5: Let Your Customers Talk to Each Other

For many businesses the idea of allowing their customers to interact online together sounds like a complete nightmare. In my opinion the real problem isn't with the customers, but with the policies and services of the business they are discussing.

In other words the real question is, what do you have to hide?

The reality is that customers will discuss you, your products, and how they feel about them whether you like it or not. You would be wise to provide them a forum for these discussions. It's better to have a forum that you can easily monitor and use to reply to customer issues.

If you remain transparent and don't give in to hiding your flaws, then your forum could become a central hub of loyalty building activity.

Many businesses could benefit from this idea.

It's easier than ever to set up a discussion forum online where your customers can meet and discuss your products and services and how they are using them. It could be as simple as setting up a Facebook.com fan page or even a free Ning.com community.

If you are able to achieve the establishment of an active online discussion forum related to your products or services, then you will have an amazing asset that will only boost your reputation and credibility in your niche market.

# PART 2

# SIMPLE INEXPENSIVE WEBSITES YOU MIGHT NEED

The fact is, building a large informational website is where most businesses start and stop their online efforts. The Internet is clogged with these sites, as nearly every business has either put up a site themselves, or they've paid (or overpaid) to have a web designer build one for them. You may have heard the apt analogy of billboards in the desert, and that's exactly what most informational websites are. Imagine thousands of huge beautiful billboard signs posted in the desert pointing nowhere. That is the state of the current business landscape online.

It's a sad fact, but most of the business informational sites being built are worthless for driving new business. You don't have to look far to find business owners that are unhappy with how their $5,000 to $50,000 informational websites have turned out, and they are even less pleased with how much business the site is generating for them. It's an even uglier picture when you consider the trends I talk about later on in the book, regarding mobile marketing and how our cell phone screens are forcing the entire Internet to fit on a small and simple screen. In other words, you'd better have a good reason for building a big, pretty website, because most of them are a waste of space.

## TOUGH QUESTIONS

How profitable is your informational site? Is it helping you grow your business? If not, why not? If so, how can you improve your online efforts?

Having a website stuffed full of general facts and information about your business does serve a purpose, but it is also a never-ending project that can be a distraction and actually hurt your online efforts if not done right.

Why do these types of monolith sites get built? My theory is that many web design firms love building these types of sites because of the massive potential billable hours they'll book in doing so. It's also a matter of management pride at times, I think. It's a mentality that says, "He who has the biggest, fanciest website wins."

## A HARSH REALITY

Being a great web designer is entirely different from being a good web marketer. I've met only a handful of people in my life that were decent at both and I've yet to meet someone that is great at both. If you want to make money you want someone with a marketing mindset in charge of your website efforts—not someone with a designer mindset.

It's typically a waste of time to build a large, expensive site that tells clients all the pitch facts about your business, such as how long you've been in business, what your core skills are, who your employees are, how wonderful you are compared to your competition, what your business looks like, what management thinks of the future of your industry, and so on. All of this makes for a boring space.

So, what *does* work online?

If we can agree that the primary purpose of a website is to generate leads, make sales, move prospects continually closer to the point of doing business with you, and build loyalty, then I hope to convince you that building small, focused sites that engage and connect with prospects is the way to go. These simple sites can be built on a tiny budget, and can produce amazing results. Your customers and business instincts will tell you when it's time to build more complex sites because you won't be able to live without them (if that point ever comes).

Before building any website be sure to answer some basic who, what, where, and why questions.

- Who is the site targeted at and who is in charge of making sure it reaches that target?
- What content do customers/prospects want on the site?
- Where are the leads and prospects that will be using the site and how will it be marketed to those people?
- Why is the site necessary?

- What customers or prospects can we identify that are virtually demanding this site be built?
- How will it grow your business?

Let's take a look at what simple websites work well.

# CHAPTER 7

# LEAD CAPTURE PAGES AND SQUEEZE PAGES

I love to see my clients build a good squeeze page because I think it's one of the most effective websites you can ever build.

Why is it so powerful? E-mail marketing is widely considered to be the most powerful form of marketing in use today. When done right the return on investment (ROI) is 50:1. I've had plenty of months where my own personal ROI was far higher than that. This means for every $1 I spend growing and managing my mailing list I can expect to put at least $50 in the bank.

In Part 13 we discuss e-mail marketing in more depth and I show you how simple e-mail campaigns can grow any business inexpensively and virtually risk-free. A squeeze page is a great way to allow targeted prospects to join your e-mail list in a systematic autopilot way, and for this reason it's one of my favorite simple sites.

So what is a squeeze page and how is it different from an informational website?

A squeeze page is a simple one page website that you've likely seen before. The entire purpose behind this site is to generate e-mail leads. One of my squeeze pages can be seen at SilentJim.com. I use this site in many ways, but here are a few examples.

- When I do radio interviews, write a guest article for a blog, comment on other people's blogs, participate on forums, and so on I always sign off by making mention of that website.
- When someone asks what I do for a living, or if they ask for a business card I send them to that site. It's the gateway to a establishing a business relationship with me.

- If I were to send first-time prospects to a page full of random facts and sales pitches trying to sell something, I would have far lower retention and far fewer sales ultimately.

## Components of a Good Squeeze Page:

- An easy to spell and hard to misspell domain name.
- The entire page fits easily on one screen. No scrolling required.
- Give something of high-perceived value away for free in exchange for a lead.
- Short bullet-point benefits about the value of opting-in are clearly stated.
- Make sure the prospect knows that you'll be sending them regular, relevant information (this can all be set up one time and put on autopilot).

Once you have an e-mail lead, the follow-up process should be automatic as you deliver the information you promised instantly. This should not be a manual process. The real power of capturing these leads is that you can give each new prospect exactly what they signed up for. Next, you can begin dripping short, informational e-mails to them over time and slowly win them over while convincing them of your expertise. Focus on educating and giving away quality relevant information. That is how the relationship will grow.

I add hundreds of new e-mail leads into my online businesses daily, and each of these valued prospects flows smoothly into the appropriate follow-up campaign designed to convert them into customers. As prospects are converted into customers, they flow from one list to another list seamlessly so that they only get appropriate correspondence from me. A good e-mail management tool will manage all of this for you.

## Tough Question: How Do I Build a Squeeze Page on a Low Budget and without Technical Skills?

The below link directs you to a YouTube video that shows you a virtually free way to get a squeeze page set up today even if you have no technical skills.

Reference: OfflineBiz.com/FreeSqueezeVideo.html

The leads generated from your squeeze page should be stored in an online e-mail management solution designed to automate the entire process for a few dollars per month. My list of well over 100,000 e-mail contacts is managed by such a service for around $100 per month. It's the best $100 I spend each month because my ROI is off the charts. I only log into my e-mail management service to check the statistics because every other aspect of it is on complete autopilot. When you are just starting out your e-mail list growth efforts you'll have to pay far less than I do.

Visit the resource page 101FreeMarketing.com and look for *E-mail Lead Management* for the most current information on this topic as well as my currently preferred e-mail lead management tools.

Other sections of this book cover generating prospects online and e-mail lead management, but for even more in-depth training on this subject I have an entire online video course at ListBuildingClass.com.

# CHAPTER 8

# A SALES PAGE CLOSES THE DEAL FOR YOU

**I**f your business plans include being able to sell products directly over the Internet, then you are going to need to know a bit about sales pages. Any web designer can install Buy Now buttons and a shopping cart, but I've learned a few general rules that will help you get started in building pages that actually help you make the sale.

- A good sales page does a minimum of three things: It tells the customer what exactly is being offered, explains the benefits and features, and then makes it easy for the customer to order it.
- The more detailed information you provide, such as including specifications, full shipping details if applicable, multiple payment options, and so on, the better off you'll be. Providing maximum information puts your customer at ease. I'm a big fan of long, detailed sales pages.
- When writing a sales letter for any product, remember to address the product from the customer's vantage point. While there is some value in listing the features of a product being sold, it is far more valuable to list the benefits from the customer's perspective.
- Include customer testimonials. What others are saying about you is far more relevant to prospects than what you are saying about yourself.
- Include plenty of detailed pictures if applicable.
- Make it easy for the customer to contact you off-line. Having a toll-free number or a live chat feature installed on any sales page will almost certainly help the conversion rate and will rarely hinder it. You can have your own toll-free number set up in minutes very inexpensively using an online service like twilio.com. A phone number is crucial if you have a higher price point product.

- Include certifications, trust seals, or Better Business Bureau logos that your business has earned. This will also help make the sale.
- Offer several options for payment. If you don't have a merchant account consider Paypal.com as your payment service. It's cheap and easy to set up, commonly accepted, and your customers don't have to have a PayPal account of their own in order to pay you through their system with any major credit card. The buttons that PayPal gives you access to are easily dropped onto any website. The buttons can easily be customized to include a "Thank You" page for post-ordering communication. This simple solution is the best place to start for most small businesses in my opinion. I've done tens of thousands of transactions on PayPal and remain a big fan of their services.
- The most effective sales pages are isolated, stand-alone pages that contain full detail on the one product being sold. Don't put distractions and unrelated links all over a sales page. Make it focused and strategically aimed at one purpose—making the sale.
- By all means you should be testing the conversion rate on virtually every page on your website, especially your sales pages. Split testing virtually every aspect of your conversion process online will reap huge rewards. The basics of split testing are pretty simple to grasp. Once you have an established baseline conversion rate on any given website, the next step is to divert some of your incoming traffic to a nearly identical test page that has just one different feature, such as a varied headline or different background color. Once you have significant statistical evidence to show that the baseline page is outperformed by your test page, you should upgrade your baseline page and then continue trying to establish a new baseline by introducing new test pages constantly. I cover split testing a bit more in Part 20.

# CHAPTER 9

# A COMMUNITY SITE BUILDS YOUR AUDIENCE AND INCREASES LOYALTY

**O**ne of the most powerful websites you can invest your time and energy into is one that you probably don't even have to build yourself when you are first starting out. Once your audience is more established, though, you'll have to strongly consider having a community page of your own. This could be anything from a Facebook fan page, to a thriving multi-department forum/discussion board, or even a free ning.com community site.

A community page is where your customers can gather and ideally discuss with each other and with you the issues, concerns, and helpful tips regarding products and ideas related to your business. It isn't always possible to have an active, targeted discussion forum if there isn't significant niche interest, but if you can succeed in establishing an active community online you'll enjoy rich benefits.

The start of the process in establishing such a forum is identifying the personas (or multiple personas) of your typical client base. Are they young or old? Are they male or female? What income, education, and hobbies might they have? Identifying these target traits will help you narrow down your search and will help make your marketing efforts as targeted as possible. Once you know who it is you are looking for, you can then go hang out online where they hang out. By using tact, being helpful, and establishing trust (this all can take some time), you'll earn the right to be followed.

I encourage most of my students and clients to begin their online marketing efforts by identifying and participating in the forums where their target customer base is already hanging out. Just be a member. If you can't find an active blog, discussion forum, group, membership website, or other online destination where your target prospects gather in large numbers, then you are likely in an uphill battle to generate interest in the product or service that you are selling by using an online community-related approach.

Consider my membership website as an example of how this is all supposed to work.

One of my most popular websites is a place where hundreds of online entrepreneurs gather daily and openly discuss establishing and growing their multiple online revenue streams. I've invited multiple expert guest contributors to offer up their ideas and creative strategies to our paid membership base. We have established a virtual library of courses and topics on various income strategies. Everyone involved benefits from this arrangement. Frequently one of my invited guest experts will share a product, message, or website that really resonates with part of my membership base.

Under the old rules of doing business I should probably be nervous when my customers get excited and drawn away to another website by someone else's expertise and offers, but in this case I'm not nervous at all because I've built a network of strong relationships that are mutually beneficial in every direction. In effect, I've built a large audience that trusts my ability and instincts, and a large Rolodex of experts that return the favors I've given them. My site has become a proving ground of ideas and experts, and I openly invite both inside.

Many newbie experts have established themselves by drawing away the attention of a portion of my audience, but in return I've established my own credibility, expanded my Rolodex of available experts, and provided my audience with fantastic content. I also know that if the newbie expert goes on to thrive that I'll reap the benefit of having them rave to others about who helped them get started (me).

It all comes back to having a community and establishing a position of influence inside of that community.

The formula might look something like this:

$$CI = PA \times ET \times SA \times DO$$

- Community Influence (CI): The relative measure of your ability to trigger a response or a course of action among a group of followers.
- Perceived Authority (PA): To what degree does the group overall consider you to be an authority? Use a scale of 1 to 10 if it helps, with 10 being the ultimate authority.
- Established Trust (ET): Trust takes time to establish, but can be lost in an instant. Again, use a scale of 1 to 10 and try to get into the mind

of your community. How much do they trust you? How can you earn more of it?

- Size of Audience (SA): Obviously, the larger the audience the bigger your influence score will be. A larger, more loyal audience is the goal.
- Degree of Ownership (DO): While participating in someone else's forum area is certainly beneficial when setting out to establish your own trust and credibility, and you may find that this position suits you just fine for the long term, ultimately the most benefit comes from having your own forum area that you can fully control on your own. (Full Ownership = 3, Partial Ownership (moderator, resident expert etc.) = 2, Little Ownership = 1).

I think you'll find this formula helpful if you use it to try to establish the highest value possible for CI. To increase your CI score, take steps to increase your PA, EA, SA, and DO (even being a frequent contributor does this for you).

Community influence of course is a relative term, but that doesn't make it impossible to track your progress by working on any of these factors.

Once you are in a position of authority or ownership inside a community, one of the most valuable roles you can play is to constantly be finding and inviting in other complementary experts. As these new experts and other forum members prove themselves to be true leaders, be sure to promote them to higher levels of ownership. In other words, increase their DO score for them to keep them loyal and feeling rewarded for that loyalty.

Tim Kerber is the current owner of MemberGate software. His software is used to manage a great number of membership website communities, including two of my sites that have a total combined membership of over 10,000 members. In conversations with him while I was establishing my first membership site, he emphasized to me that the best indicator of long-term success for any membership site is the health and commitment level of members inside of the discussion forum area. A discussion forum that only has an occasional post from an occasional member is not active enough to establish your influence, but an active forum with dozens, hundreds, or more visitors daily is obviously going to lead to great things for you and your business.

Want to set up a robust community of your own for free? Check out ning.com

# CHAPTER 10

# BLOGGING FOR CUSTOMERS

I haven't seen any statistics on the subject, but I can venture a guess with great certainty on the matter all the same. I would estimate that somewhere around 90 percent of all blogs aren't being read by anyone other than the author and perhaps a small number of other readers.

Starting a blog just because you can, or just because you want to will not lead to great things in and of itself.

In other parts of this book I discuss how to grow a loyal audience and following online. Once you have started to establish a loyal online following it makes sense to start a blog, but until then you'll likely find it difficult to grow a following by blogging alone. While there are some success stories that started with a blog, most of the time other traffic and publicity generation efforts were required.

So who needs a blog anyway?

For me and many other successful online marketers and businesses, a blog or blog type of web page serves as a gathering point for the community of readers and followers that are interested in the content that the expert regularly posts.

If you, or someone in your organization, is ready to commit to the task of engaging with your prospects by creating relevant information on a regular basis, then it's time for a blog.

Your blog is the home base of your activity. It is a history of your progress, a gathering place for your most loyal followers, and potentially a great income stream for your business as your audience grows.

## BLOGGING OPTIONS

I'm a big fan of using WordPress to create a blog. There are thousands of plug-ins that can be easily applied to your blog to make it have the look and functionality that you want. You can find experts all over the world familiar with the WordPress platform, and it's not hard to turn a WordPress site into a very nice looking website with very little effort. The odds are that you've been on several WordPress sites in the past month without even realizing it because they are so easy to customize into a non-blog looking site.

Tumblr.com is also used to quickly create great-looking blogs by millions of people worldwide. Perhaps the most popular feature of Tumblr that sets them apart is the ability to re-blog. According to the Tumblr supplied definition, re-blogging happens the same way that YouTube uses embedding to make it easy for a video to become a viral hit. Any Tumblr blogger can click the re-blog button on any other blogger's post, thereby helping to spread the original post across multiple blogs very quickly.

## What to Blog About

I spend time discussing how to distinguish yourself and provide valuable content in other sections of this book, so I won't write much about it here. But the easiest way to sum up what should go into your blog is to say this:

"Write about things that your audience wants to read about and do it with passion and personality."

## Blog Features

I'm not too concerned about the layout, graphics, or overall marketing appeal of your blog. These are not the things that serious prospects and readers will actually care all that much about *unless* you go way overboard. You can also look too cheap and thrown together, but let's assume you know how to recognize that when you see it.

The success of your blog is based upon the quality of the content and your ability to draw readers to your blog. Once you are convinced of this reality then you're ready to add in a few key features that will make your blog the best marketing machine it can be.

**Here are some features that will make your blog easy to use as well as a powerful marketing machine:**
- All of the content that you add to your blog should go into a handful of categories that are easily accessed by the reader.
- You may not choose the same favorite articles that your audience does.
- You'd be wise to pay attention to the types of articles that generate the most comments and feedback and then highlight those articles by making them easy to access in their own category, and then provide

more of that type of content to your readers. A category such as "Most Talked About" will get a lot more clicks than a category named "Articles from 2007." If the readers aren't saying anything, that is also a very clear message. Any decent blog developer can easily assist you in adding in tools or plug-ins that will automate the placement of popular articles into a most popular articles category. Base your other categories around the content that seems to be the most popular to your readers. Let the readers lead.

- Have a *Press* category where members of the media can quickly get everything they need about you and your business. Engage in media stalking, as discussed in Chapter 28, and actively promote the Press area on your blog.

- Unless a dated timeline is necessary for the organization of your content, don't include a bunch of archived years and months in the side margin of your blog. Few people will care how long you've been blogging.

- Try to make your content as evergreen as possible. This means make it relevant for as long as possible without time stamping it. Once a blog visitor gets the feeling that they are reading outdated information they will lose interest very quickly. Consider eliminating dates or dated events entirely from your blogging activities. Those types of articles belong in a newsletter.

- You must make it easy for your blog visitors to leave you comments and feedback. Several blogs, including my own, now offer the ability for readers to comment not only on the article itself but also on the comments left by other readers. You should encourage and engage in these discussions to build loyalty among your audience.

- Anything that makes your content easy for readers to share among their network of contacts should be considered. For example, I include a button from tweetmeme.com inside all of my blog posts so that my readers can instantly click and share my post with their own Twitter followers if they so choose. You can find such plug-ins for Facebook, e-mail, and so on. All of these features can easily be added to any blog.

- You should have some big goals for your blog as a lead generation machine. The best marketers consider their blogs to be a source of new leads. The best next step for your blog readers to take is to join your mailing list, so be sure to have that option available to your readers on every page of your blog. I also use friendly giveaway offers to entice and incentivize my readers towards joining the mailing list.

# PART 3

# THE HABITS OF ONLINE MARKETING SUCCESS

Several new free marketing options are available to business owners today that just weren't around even a few years ago. Effectively spreading the word about what you have to offer may be a simple matter of adding a few new good habits into your routine. You can also easily recruit your customers and followers to participate in the process. The next three brief chapters will introduce some new ideas that should become routine to your marketing efforts.

If I could convince you to adapt three new habits it would be the simple ideas presented in these chapters. I cover the concepts in greater detail throughout the book, but I put the three of them here together in brief fashion because of the habitual effort that will be required for each one.

# CHAPTER 11

# SOCIAL MEDIA AND FREE MARKETING

Facebook, Twitter, and the other dozens of social media sites are still a bit of a mystery to most businesses. While there are plenty of books and training courses on the subject, most businesses still feel like they are in experimental mode, at best, when it comes to their social media marketing efforts.

In Part 12 of this book I cover social media marketing in more detail, but this chapter is a brief reminder that it is worth the effort to put your business on Facebook, Twitter, and other social marketing sites *only* if you can make it a habit. An effective social media marketing effort is not a one-time program or effort that can be assigned to one staff member. It has to become part of your culture and it may not pay big dividends overnight. Committing to social media marketing means committing to a new level of intimacy with your prospects and customers. Success relies on many of the same factors that make any relationship work—time, effort, and attention to "the little things" as you build a genuine authentic relationship with those most interested in your products, services, or message.

The good news is that you can start anytime you'd like, and it's free. Many of the most creative and inspirational success stories in business have their roots in social media. It's time to start learning the basics and then get in the habit of being there—even if you start slowly.

# CHAPTER 12

# BREVITY IS A
# MARKETING SKILL

**W**e can all agree that today's prospects and customers are more distracted than ever. To have any chance of getting your message across in such an environment, you'd better be brief. However, being brief is a skill that many people lack. It is a new habit that you will have to practice in order to perfect.

Even while writing this book I've attempted to keep my paragraphs short. My high school English teacher probably wouldn't approve, but I've learned the hard way that long paragraphs rarely get read.

Videos that are too long don't get watched. Keep them under two to three minutes, unless absolutely necessary to go longer.

E-mail messages that are more than a few sentences don't get replied to.

Voicemail messages that are longer than a few seconds get deleted.

Even the 140 characters that Twitter gives you for each new message is too much! If you want to be "retweeted" you'll have to keep your messages to 110 characters so that others can pass along your wisdom without having to edit or shorten your message.

# CHAPTER 13

# VIDEOS, PICTURES, AND TESTIMONIALS WORK MARKETING MAGIC

**W**hether you like it or not, most businesses are going to become increasingly reliant on online marketing efforts in order to sustain or grow their businesses. The best word that captures all the stuff that goes online to represent you and what you are all about is content. Even if you aren't sure what your approach to success online might be, now is the time to start capturing potential content.

Get in the habit of capturing pictures, videos, and audios of anything related to your business. Get comfortable talking to a video camera about what it is you do. Get comfortable asking customers for testimonials. Begin recording the conversations (when appropriate) where you talk passionately about why you do what you do. Be prepared to record useful telephone calls that might be beneficial to your online audience (with all parties aware of the recording of course). All of this is golden content that can be put to good use online.

You could find new prospects online simply by posting a few videos to YouTube.com talking about why you do what you do. Being authentic and passionate about what you do can lead to great things, and since most companies still aren't jumping in, get in the game now. There are no major expenses involved with capturing and sharing your content. There is no downside risk, and the potential upside is huge.

Once you capture it, you have to share it!

## VIDEO

Without any help from me (short of loaning him my handheld Flip video camera) my 10-year-old son started putting videos on YouTube.com about a year ago. The videos are simple, unedited shots of him riding his skateboard around our driveway or doing card tricks. He's just "doing what he does" while talking about it. Jump forward a year later and he has multiple videos on YouTube.com that have been viewed over 100,000 times. While he has no monetization plans (yet) for all this exposure, there is a lesson for all of us. Would your business benefit in any way in the next year if you had over 100,000 people watching you "do what you do" on YouTube.com and then talk about it? If you see the benefit, then why haven't you gotten into the habit of sharing video content yet? Will you get thousands of viewers? Maybe and maybe not, but what's the risk of trying?

## SIMPLE VIDEO SUCCESS STORY

One of my newsletter readers, Tracy Hanes, harnessed the power of on-line video as a marketing tool when he founded his consulting company a couple years ago.

Within a short time he had several major clients approaching him and he landed hundreds of thousands of dollars in business training within months.

His only strategy?

Post simple videos on YouTube.com using keywords related to his niche market in the description. These videos quickly showed up on Google for the desirable keywords that he had used in his descriptions.

He produced all the videos himself with no editing except the basic editing features of his inexpensive handheld Flip and Kodak video cameras. The video content is as simple as a guy sitting at his desk talking to an inexpensive video camera.

I asked Tracy what his secrets were in gaining so much attention from the right people with his videos and he told me, "I target keywords and do some research. I could literally pick a Google page and place a video there to get first page listing thanks to the power of video."

It's worth noting that none of Tracy's videos have gone viral—attracting thousands or millions of viewers—but, nonetheless, they have been highly effective. The several example videos he sent me had been viewed only a few dozen times each on YouTube.com, but they were working for him very well as they were bringing him the exact kinds of viewers he needed!

The results?

Tracy's business has grown in two years to include three key officers and their business in the most recent year is 1,200 percent larger than their first successful year.

Tracy's Zero Injury Institute was established in order to provide Safety Leadership Concepts and services to companies in the Industrial Safety niche.

## PICTURES

Encourage your employees, customers, and anyone involved with your business to capture and send you pictures related to your business. A good picture that captures you doing what you do can be used in multiple ways. Pictures can be uploaded to multiple free sites online along with a description and soon you'll see multiple benefits from the exposure you can get.

It could be as simple as posting a sign in your business requesting that customers send you images (even a cell phone image) of you doing what you do, or of customers using your products.

Get those pics posted where they can be seen. Pics make great content online and there are many great uses that I talk about more in this book.

Here's a quick tip: Check out animoto.com (currently a free service) and upload several of your best pics to their site in just minutes. Click a button and they create an amazing animated show that you can proudly display.

## TESTIMONIALS

Do you have any raving fans or customers that love what you do? Have you asked them for a testimonial in writing yet? Once you have it—*share it*!

From a marketer's perspective those testimonials are the equivalent of gold. I tell my staff that every testimonial we get from our fans or customers easily puts a minimum of $1,000 in our pocket. That's how much attention we pay to capturing anything positive that anyone has to say about us, but we don't ever let these great stories go stale. Frequently, we get them posted online the same day we get them.

No matter what your plans are online, having testimonials from your top fans and customers is vital to solidifying your message. Get in the habit of posting those stories where others can see them.

# PART 4

# STANDING OUT ONLINE

**B**y now most businesses realize that just having a website is not enough. Those with a little more insight realize that having a pretty website doesn't even really matter until you have the one most important ingredient of success online. That vital ingredient is targeted traffic.

A multibillion-dollar industry has sprung up around the concept of providing websites with the traffic and exposure they need in order to succeed. If you haven't figured it out yet, most of these companies are a complete rip-off. Some of them are good at what they do, but by no means should you just produce a blank check and then hope for results when working with companies that are promising traffic and eyeballs to your website.

Understanding a few basics will help you stand out online on your own, or make you much better equipped and prepared when hiring others to help you with your online presence.

# CHAPTER 14

# SEARCH ENGINE OPTIMIZATION SIMPLIFIED

While there are several search engines that arguably could be entered into a discussion about search engine optimization, I only refer to Google because all other search engines wish they were Google, and they are doing their best to emulate it. If anyone ever does pass Google, it's quite likely these same ideas would apply.

While there is an entire industry set up to provide Search Engine Optimization (SEO) services to help businesses and websites get ranked on online search engines like Google.com, there are precious few honest experts that will tell you that there is absolutely *no way* you can ever be assured of a good ranking online. Even if you are fortunate enough to get ranked well on Google in the short term, the odds are against you being there long term, unless you are both fortunate and focused in your efforts to maintain your rank using legitimate strategies.

I've encountered countless website owners that could have sworn they had cracked the Google code, but inevitably they've all realized a harsh reality (or soon likely will): Google is too smart to be fooled long-term. Only quality sites that meet the Google standards will be rewarded. Anyone can go from page 1 on Google to page 431 overnight. Pretending that this could never happen to you is simply inviting disaster. I've chosen not to rely on my Google rankings as a result, and neither should you in my opinion.

However, after saying all that, you should still do your best to generate the greatest amount of free traffic from Google that you possibly can.

What should you focus on in order to be rewarded by Google?

There are only two proven ways to get more "Google love":

1. Have a great site with current, user friendly, keyword-relevant information.
2. Most important, increase the number of quality pages that link to you.

In Google's own words: "Pages that we believe are important pages receive a higher PageRank and are more likely to appear at the top of the search results. Webmasters can improve the rank of their sites by *increasing the number of high-quality sites* that link to their pages."

What is PageRank?

The PageRank metric used by Google is assigned to virtually every publicly accessible page online. You can measure the level of importance that Google assigns to any page by checking its page rank (PR). The score is a publicly viewable number from 0 to 10, with most sites having a score of 0 or 1. You can easily add a Google PageRank indicator to your browser button bar and begin noticing the difference between sites that Google likes and sites that they barely even notice. It has nothing to do with how "slick" or pretty the site is. It has everything to do with protecting the user experience when Google users enter a search phrase. Google wants the best of the best websites at the top. The best information, most up to date, most linked to, and so on.

## WHAT'S THE DIFFERENCE BETWEEN ORGANIC RESULTS AND PAID RESULTS?

Keep in mind that this entire chapter is referring to Google's "organic results." These are the websites that Google likes and rewards with a good search engine rank at no expense whatsoever to the site owner. You'll notice when using the Google.com search engine that they always list the paid results or pay-per-click ads down the right-hand side of the screen, as well as a handful of them at the top of the screen. All of these ads appear as a result of someone paying (in some cases paying a lot) to appear in those positions. There are entire books written about the expensive prospect of effectively using these ads for advertising. I don't rely on pay-per-click ads, and this book won't be discussing them very much at all, because the learning curve is typically expensive when using them and the title of this book is "Free Marketing."

Get more information on Google PageRank by searching Google for the term "page rank." Your efforts at increasing your level of respect from

Google can easily be tracked by watching your score slowly creep up over time.

How does Google's algorithm really work?

To truly understand what you are up against when trying to win the affections of Google you'll need to start to grasp how seriously they take the business of ranking websites. One of their core missions is to automate, as much as possible, the process of providing easy access to the best content on the Internet for all users of Google.com. Once you understand that core service is their goal, consider the fact that they've spent countless hours and millions of dollars hiring the most brilliant statisticians, mathematicians, genius-level data analysts, and so on, all chartered with the mission of creating a top-secret algorithm that automatically tracks and assigns page rank scores to every website online, and then decides which sites will appear on which pages of the organic search results.

Yes—it's that complicated.

Want it all broken down in simple terms?

One of the best explanations I've ever heard of the Google ranking algorithm is this:

Imagine a large wall covered with light switches. There are rows and rows, each with hundreds of light switches. Several top secret, genius-level engineers are assigned the task of continually adjusting those light switches in such a way that the Google search engine performs at an optimum level. It is an ongoing process that never stabilizes. The process never stabilizes because Google does not want anyone to know the exact nature of their algorithm. They don't want anyone to be able to manipulate their machine. I even have a theory (my opinion only) that there are several random elements in this process that make it impossible to fully map out by anyone ... ever (even their own engineers).

The next time someone tells you that they can guarantee you results on Google, imagine that person matching wits with the multimillion-dollar genius-level process I've just described. While there is a chance that they might be able to accomplish some results some of the time in the short term, the only long-term strategy that might work is to play by the rules. This means creating unique, quality content that other quality websites will willingly (and voluntarily) link to. The process of having other sites link to yours is called creating back links. If anyone tells you they can automate the process of creating great back links you should know that they are participating in a process that Google is actively spending millions of dollars and many genius-level man hours trying to punish. Again, it's worth repeating: Google cannot be fooled. They will find the best websites and reward them, and they will find the sites that have automated the manipulation of their system and they will punish them.

# CHAPTER 15

# KEYWORD MARKETING

Nearly all businesses have been impacted by the consumer habit of researching online before making virtually any purchase or major decision. Customers are researching online more now than ever before.

How can you get in front of these online prospects?

In order to attract the types of prospects that your business needs you'll need to know your keywords. While I won't go into all the technical details in one chapter, I can give you 90 percent of what you'll ever need to know about identifying the keywords that your prospects are using to try to find you. Once you know these keywords you are better equipped to do what it takes to make sure you or your business comes up online as being related to these keywords.

Knowing your keywords isn't enough, nor is it enough to just stuff your top keywords all over your website. Make no mistake in thinking this is a simple process, nor is it a process that you can take the write-a-check approach with to make it go away. Having a top-rated website that consistently appears high in the natural search engine results is a matter of ongoing commitment to relevance, incoming links, and steady content development.

The keywords associated with your business are the words that potential prospects are using to search Google or other search engines as they begin to research a buying decision that will eventually (hopefully) lead them to you. Odds are you already know instinctively what many of these keywords are, but inevitably there will be several keywords that you can't come up with on your own that you'll need to be aware of. Next are a couple of great tools to help you identify them.

# GOOGLE'S FREE KEYWORD TOOL

If you search Google for the phrase "keyword tool" you'll see a link to the free keyword tool that can be used by anyone. Currently the tool is located here:

adwords.Google.com/select/KeywordToolExternal

By typing in a few obvious keywords or phrases into this tool you will be given a long list of other related keywords and phrases that are being used by online searchers both locally and around the world.

Another great thing about this tool is that it will show you how many searches are being performed both locally and worldwide for various keywords and phrases related to your business. It's a good way to gauge how much search engine activity there is for any given keyword, phrase, or niche market.

Once you have this information at your disposal one, of the most powerful actions you can take is to make a practice of using your keywords and phrases in strategic ways online. Sprinkling the keywords and phrases inside your blog or websites or in the descriptions for any other content you create such as videos or audios will go a long way towards garnering you the attention of the search engines. Even using your keywords and phrases when naming the pictures that you post on your website can help your search engine rank.

### YouTube as a Keyword Tool

Check out this website:

https://ads.YouTube.com/keyword_tool

Since YouTube is the second-largest search site online (and it's owned by Google as well), it only makes sense that it would have its own keyword tool.

### Power Tools
**Two of my favorite powerful keyword opportunity-finding software tools are:**
- Micro Niche Finder:
    www.micronichefinder.com/index.htm
- Market Samurai:
    www.marketsamurai.com

## CHAPTER 16

# GET FOUND ON SEARCH ENGINES

**A**s mentioned earlier, the non-advertisement links that appear first on Google or any other major search engine are referred to as the organic results.

Having your website pages appear among the top few organic links that appear on Google can be a huge boost to the traffic that your website receives. While I don't ever rely solely on such positioning in my own businesses, or in the businesses of my clients, it is certainly beneficial to take advantage of the opportunity to achieve such a position using legitimate strategies.

**Here are some creative and legitimate ways to improve your site's rank on Google:**
- Leave legitimate blog comments on popular blogs related to your niche. As part of your useful and relevant comment be sure to include a link to your site. Most blog owners have a comment feature set up that includes a field where the commenting visitor can indicate the location of their website. This will all happen naturally as you follow the blogs of other experts and websites related to your niche.
- Volunteer to be a guest blogger on sites where you have something useful to contribute. Include links to your site in the signature line of the articles.
- Have a Facebook fan page or Twitter.com account and include links to your sites in your posts and in your bio.
- Submit articles to popular article hosting sites or press release sites. Do a search on Google for "article distribution," or "press release" for more information.

- Approach other sites in your niche with similar Google page rank and agree to swap links to help you both improve your position. Don't automate this process or pay for links, or you'll be playing with fire that could get you burned. The older, and the higher the PageRank of the site that you are swapping links with, the better. Start a list of several targeted sites that you'd like to swap links with and then actively target someone at each of those sites and build a relationship with them. A partnership with high profile websites will have many mutually benefits.
- Send heartfelt testimonials to your favorite services online and include your website domain name and picture as part of your signature. As I've become more successful online I make a habit of sending useful, genuine testimonials to the websites that provide me services. Often times these testimonials are added to these quality ranked websites, and they do me the favor of including a link to my websites along with the testimonial and picture I've sent them.

I'll repeat my basic advice about search engine optimization one more time. If you are going to pay someone to make efforts on your behalf in this area, be sure to have a good conversation with them about their understanding of Google's algorithm, and imagine that person matching wits with a system that makes it virtually impossible for long-term manipulation to occur.

# CHAPTER 17

# GOOGLE MAPS AND GOOGLE PLACES

**I**f your business serves a customer base within a given geographical region, you could greatly benefit from the exposure you'll gain from listing your business in Google Places.

Even businesses that aren't servicing a set geographical region may still benefit from being listed, but those with a geographic focus will benefit the most.

Since most customers are now using search engines to find businesses and services instead of Yellow Pages, or any other type of business directory, it only makes sense to take advantage of any free opportunity you have to get yourself listed in online directories that service businesses. By far the most popular directory is Google Places.

Rather than create a long chapter describing Google Places in detail, the best place to send you is directly to the informational page on Google itself. Visit:

places.Google.com

and click on "Places for Business" for more information on Google Places.

Alternately you can search Google for the term "Google Places."

There's nothing overly complicated about the process of getting your business listed. Over time the rules and features will inevitably change, so I won't spend a lot of time on the details in this chapter. There are several strategies you should consider, however, in order to improve your odds of ranking well in the Google Places directory when you show up listed near your competition.

# First, Let's Hear from Google

According to Google, there's not much you can do to improve your rankings in their directory, but they *do* have an algorithm at work that ranks all member businesses.

As noted in Google.com regarding Google Places and Google Maps:

"All Google search results are based primarily on relevance, and Google Maps listings are no different. Google Maps ranks business listings based on their relevance to the search terms entered, along with geographic distance (where indicated), and other factors. Sometimes our search technology decides that a business that's farther away from your location is more likely to have what you're looking for than a business that's closer.

Google Maps and Google Places are a free service, so there's no way to request or pay for a better ranking. We also can't provide additional details about our ranking algorithm. We do our best to keep the details of the algorithm confidential in order to make the ranking system as fair as possible for everyone."

So, once again there's that secret algorithm, but this time Google is leaving giant clues about how the system works. You can see these clues just by using Google.com to search for "city name + service businesses." By paying attention to the type of behavior that Google rewards, you can start to make some pretty obvious observations about how to rank well on Google Places.

The next chapter fills you in on how to improve your odds of generating maximum traffic from Google Places.

# CHAPTER 18

# FILL UP GOOGLE PLACES TO GET FOUND

We've established that Google does not like to be manipulated in their search results. Don't try to fool the system because nothing is stopping Google from removing you entirely from their directory if they detect that you are breaking even seemingly small rules unintentionally.

With that warning in mind there are several obvious steps that you can take to increase your exposure on Google Places. Mostly it involves filling up your profile with quality content and information, having multiple customers leave testimonials on common review sites, and perhaps most importantly, having an indexed website associated with your Google Places listing.

Let's examine those three concepts in order:

### First, Fill Up All Possible Fields with Good Content

This is self-explanatory, but follow the directions and be thorough. It's just like the science fair when you were a kid. It's not the guy with the best experiment who won every year. Instead, it was the kid with the most thorough report with all the blanks filled in.

### Testimonials

While you should never manipulate Google's system by attempting to generate false testimonials, you can certainly encourage your top customers to leave you feedback and reviews on the sites associated with your industry. The more positive reviews you have from various customers, the higher you will see yourself ranked in Google Places.

### Have an Indexed Website

Having an indexed website with a high PageRank score associated with your business listing is a huge boost to your ranking in Google Places. It's probably going to be the biggest factor as more and more businesses jump on board and claim their free Google Places accounts. In earlier chapters of Part 4 I showed you how to track your PageRank score. Improving the PageRank score of the website associated with your Google Places listing will almost certainly improve your Google Places listing rank.

***Some Reminders about PageRank and Indexing on Google***   Before any website is assigned a page rank by Google it must first be indexed (or found) by Google. You can quickly find out if your website has been indexed on Google (or any of the other major search engines like Yahoo! or Bing) by typing this simple search phrase into the search engine: "site:sitename.com" (no quotation marks needed). In other words, if your website is xyz.com, you can find out if you are indexed on Google by searching Google for the phrase:

site:xyz.com

If you discover that Google has not yet indexed your website, you can point it out to them in the hopes that they will index it and assign it a PageRank score. While there are no guarantees that Google will decide to index your site once they find it, this page—Google.com/addurl—is where you can go to point out a new website to Google.

Once Google has found and indexed your website, ideally they will assign a PageRank score as well. Use the other information from the chapters in this part of the book to continually build a better PageRank score with Google. The higher your PageRank score climbs, the more likely you are to be found among the first few listings in Google places when someone searches for your type of business in your area.

## GOOGLE MAPS TIP

To add Google maps to your website in any number of creative ways check out: maps.Google.com/help/maps/getmaps

# CHAPTER 19

# A Good Name Is Good Marketing

**I** did some research and quickly found one of the longest possible English surnames on record. How would you like to have the last name Featherstonehaugh? Worse yet, how would you like to be the poor guy in charge of advertising and marketing the family pool installation business for that name?

Featherstonehaugh Pools and Patios—a family business since 1886. Find us online at:

Featherstonehaughpoolsandpatios.com (Don't bother registering that website—no one will see it.)

Do you ever hear a business name on a radio spot and feel sorry for the business owner because of the terrible name that was chosen? If you have to spell it three times for me, it's a bad domain name.

Businesses today are much more likely to choose intuitive business names or domain names because more of us are recognizing the importance of keywords and ease of spelling even as part of a business name.

The search engines will also reward you for choosing website names and business names that contain good searchable keywords.

What if it's too late? What if your name is already included as part of your business name, or your business name contains no good search engine keywords? What if your current website domain name is a long ugly tangle of letters that no one ever remembers?

There are simple solutions—and you don't have to redo your website!

There is strong evidence to suggest that owning the domain name associated with your city or region as well as a strong keyword or keyword phrase can really help your rankings on the search engines as well as on Google Places. Even if you don't have immediate plans for such a domain name, now is the time to secure these types of domain names because they may become very valuable in the near future in my opinion. For example, if you live in a city named "Anytown" and you have a roofing company, you should go register the domain name "AnytownRoofing.com" immediately. It will only cost you a few dollars per year to hold on to that domain name, and trust me: you will thank me for it later. At some point you may move your entire website to the new domain name and greatly improve the look and feel of your marketing materials, but in any case, the site could be a great source of leads for you, separate from the efforts you are making on your current website.

Getting a keyword-rich domain name like AnytownRoofing.com indexed is an ideal scenario because it is yet another positive mark in your favor on the search engines.

In the next chapter I offer another simple use for a nice sounding, easy to spell, intuitive domain name.

# CHAPTER 20

# FIX YOUR BAD NAME INSTANTLY

**H**aving at least one domain name that is easy to spell and easy to remember is important. If you are currently using a poorly named domain as your flagship domain name, then you are likely missing out on a lot of potential marketing exposure and business.

I have no intention of convincing you to throw out whatever domain names you are currently using. Instead I'm going to convince you to try to find an easy to spell and easy to remember domain name or two that could be pointed at your current primary website. Nearly all registrars, such as GoDaddy.com, offer a service called "domain forwarding." If you don't have the need for an entirely new website you still could likely benefit from thinking up a new, better domain name, and then point that domain name at your current website without any extra work needed. Just use domain forwarding so you can use a better sounding name in your marketing efforts.

Instinctually we all know when a website has a bad name. We instantly forget a bad name, or worse yet we find it difficult to spell correctly based on the sound of the name. For example, including the word "to" as part of your domain name invites multiple possible spelling errors (two, too, 2) when users attempt to type the domain name into a browser.

This is especially true when you are designing a squeeze page with the intended purpose of capturing the maximum number of leads on a simple one-page website (as discussed in Chapter 7).

I realized early in my online career that I needed a good memorable domain name to refer people to when I was interviewed on the radio or in articles. I also didn't have a good central website to send people to when I met them in person at conferences or speaking engagements. At that point I established SilentJim.com. While it's not a perfect name choice, it

70

is fairly memorable and easy to spell correctly. It's also short enough that I can use it in other places as well. For example, my YouTube.com ID is "SilentJimDotCom."

Who should consider setting up a new domain name with an easy to market name?

**If you:**
- Have a website that is difficult to spell (remember my proposed business name Featherstonehaughpoolsandpatios.com—don't be like them, please!). Have a domain name that contains words that sound alike but can be spelled differently, such as "four" (for, fore, 4). Are seeking to attract e-mail leads via a squeeze page. Have a long domain name and need a shorter, more memorable one for advertising purposes. Are currently using a long, ugly link, or a subdomain as your primary website (for example, yoursite.hostsite.com/mypage.html).
- Have a popular page or feature of your website that you want to be able to send visitors or prospects to directly without them having to navigate through your main website.
- Have business cards, brochures, outdoor signage, bumper stickers, etc., that contain a website name with a dot in the middle or a slash in it.

If you have any of these issues, you are a good candidate for a new domain name.

As inexpensive and easy as it is to register a new domain name and point that name at any site, I'm often surprised by how many people are still promoting long, ugly, hard-to-spell domain names in their marketing efforts.

# CHAPTER 21

# ONLINE VIDEO AS A LEAD GENERATOR

**H**ere's a quick question for you. Can you name the top four search engines online? Unless you included YouTube.com on your list, you'd be incorrect.

YouTube has now firmly established itself as far more than just a random video hosting site. It is now a viable search engine for an unimaginable amount of topical video-based content. The best part of all is that it's 100 percent free to use, and to upload content to.

If you aren't putting yourself on YouTube, you aren't in the game as much as you should be.

I told you in Chapter 13 about my son, who has been able to gather hundreds of thousands of views and thousands of followers on his YouTube account without any help from me. He didn't set out to accomplish these things; he just turned on a video camera and recorded himself doing what he does. His spelling is atrocious, he doesn't try to use the right keywords, and he has no idea why all of it is getting so big so fast. My point is, if a 10-year-old with a borrowed $100 video camera can create a virtual empire online, why aren't you getting your message out on YouTube?

As with all highly trafficked sites, my advice is typically the same. Be authentic, be creative, and generate leads into your sales funnel by providing valuable content and advice. YouTube is no exception.

In most of the videos that I put on YouTube, I will have a very gentle call to action at some point in the video. This call to action invites the viewer to join my e-mail mailing list typically. Sometimes I giveaway free downloadable information products as part of the video presentation as well. I don't always have a business purpose in mind when putting content on YouTube, however. One of my most watched videos is one that shows how to get a high score on a fun, online paper airplane game. With the tens of thousands of viewers that I've received to my paper airplane video, I'm sure some of them have noticed my other videos as well.

From a marketing perspective, I find that the most powerful videos are the ones that let you in to the real world of the person making the video. Once again, I'm talking about being authentic. Some of the most popular content on YouTube is the simple stuff. These are the videos that make it easy for the viewer to connect and relate with the maker of the video. Using too many slick graphics, intros, great backgrounds, and so on, can actually work against you depending on what your purpose is. This should be encouraging to those who are nervous about creating video content. Spend some time on YouTube checking out popular videos on topics related to your niche interest. You'll quickly see what I mean about the authentic videos rising to the top.

In Part 10 I cover using video in greater detail.

# CHAPTER 22

# HOW TO FOOL GOOGLE AND WIND UP ON TOP EVERY TIME

It still amazes me the number of people that are completely gullible when it comes to buying into the hype and promises made by those that claim they can beat Google. These unscrupulous companies and so-called experts claim that they can get your website or business ranked high on the Google search engine for the right price. Google Maps and Google Places are just as protected by Google as is their search engine.

Let's get one thing clear.

Google, as a company, is collectively *far* smarter than anyone who is trying to manipulate their system.

The sooner you realize that, the better off you'll be.

If you haven't figured it out yet, I intentionally made the title of this chapter a bit deceiving just so I could take this opportunity to warn you and remind you (like I did in Chapter 14) about just how smart Google really is.

Google has poured hundreds of millions (or possibly billions) into protecting the integrity and end-user experience in regards to their search engine. They won't tolerate anyone with a secret formula to start bumping off the best and most deserving websites and businesses from page one of their results.

Do you want to be on page one of Google for your top keywords or business specific geographical searches?

Here's how you can do it every time:

Be worthy of being on page one of Google, and then keep doing whatever it takes to continue to be worthy. That's how you improve your odds of getting there and staying there.

That advice sort of sounds a lot like what you have to do to be on top in any endeavor, doesn't it? There just aren't any short cuts that will get you recognized as being fantastic in the long term. The only way to get that sort of recognition is to be fantastic at what you do. The recognition will come.

If you are ever approached by an SEO or consulting business that promises you results on Google, or if they want to automate the process of making you look good to Google, beware! You are wise to be very leery of what steps someone wants to take to fool Google or any other major player (Bing.com, Yahoo.com, or even YouTube.com). It's your website and your brand so you have to be the one to protect it. You simply don't want Google on your bad side. I could give you lists of names of people that have tried to manipulate Google and wound up having their site entirely deleted from the Google index. Their website wasn't deleted, but Google removed their site from the search results that appear when users search Google. I don't want this to happen to you and, trust me, Google does this hundreds, if not thousands, of times every day to people and websites that they feel are gaming the system. There is no recourse. There is no toll-free support phone number. You are just out of the game at that point.

I've chosen not to rely at all on Google as a source of traffic for my online efforts. They are too big, too powerful, and too unpredictable. I do enjoy seeing them send me some traffic when it happens, but I certainly don't plan my business around whatever they happen to send me in any given month.

# PART 5

# Draw Your Business on a Napkin

**N**ot that long ago, the first step to starting any business was to write up a business plan. But now, along with resumes, brand awareness campaigns, mass-media advertising, and phones with cords, the traditional business plan is slowly becoming irrelevant and unnecessary for more business start-ups, as well as established businesses that are looking to change course.

I like to keep things simple.

If you can draw a funnel and then describe the persona of your ideal client, you have laid the basic foundation for any business you are trying to market.

# CHAPTER 23

# WANT MORE LEADS NOW?
# DRAW A FUNNEL

**P**erhaps the biggest breakthrough moment for my online business was when I took the time to draw a funnel of my business lead management process, and then filled in each layer of the funnel with the types of products and prospects that belonged in each layer.

If I had gaps in my funnel drawing, I set about filling those gaps methodically.

The most resilient businesses in the Internet age will be the businesses that can complete this exercise and then constantly improve and expand their funnel.

I first learned the funnel concept from some training I received from Dan Kennedy.

To do this exercise you start out by drawing a Y-shaped funnel that is wider at the top and narrower at the bottom. Next, draw three or four evenly spaced horizontal lines through your funnel.

Each level you create as you move down represents a better kind of customer for your business. As you move down the funnel, the products you provide customers at each level become more exclusive and these customers are more willing to invest with you. The level of intimacy increases as the crowd shrinks as you move down the funnel.

Obviously the goal is to increase the number of prospects flowing into the top of the funnel, and preserve as many of those leads as possible as you move them through the funnel. The speed that you move them through the funnel is another valuable metric, but ideally we are going after lifelong prospects, so time is not the most urgent factor. If you can automate the process of moving the prospects along, then you are even better off.

The chapters in this book about e-mail marketing will help with that process.

Let's dissect the funnel.

The top of your funnel is where your introductory and free products are used to attract prospects. Ideally these products are high-value information products that you can giveaway to grow loyalty and earn the respect of your prospects. Not everyone that accepts this free information will move down the funnel to the next level, but you should continually improve your offers, and continually improve the quality of the content that you are willing to giveaway, in order to keep the lead flow steady.

Once a customer makes a small move in your direction by buying a low end product, or by making further inquiries, they move to the next level.

I'm forced to speak in general terms about all of this because I want it to apply to as many different business models as possible, but let's dissect one of my business funnels a bit to illustrate how this works in real life.

The top of my offer funnel consists of free videos on YouTube or on my own websites, free downloadable reports, and free newsletters that both educate and assist those looking to establish or grow a home-based or small business online. While I'm educating my prospects I gently inform them of my low-priced services, such as inexpensive courses, e-books, and paid reports that are relevant to the topics being discussed. Those customers that choose to make an initial purchase continue to receive great free content, but they are also introduced to my membership sites and coaching programs. At each level the customer loyalty and the price points increase, while the pool of participants shrinks. The most serious students wind up working closely with me.

In all cases the top of the funnel is best filled with quality content and information products that help establish your credibility and expertise while giving customers just what they were looking for. All of this is done well before you try to make a sale.

Besides just using free strategies to bring leads into your sales funnel, you can also experiment with paid advertising strategies. This is my adaptation of another sales funnel lesson I picked up from Dan Kennedy.

In this book I've shown you multiple free lead generation strategies, but imagine that you have three paid sources of leads available to you as well. Should you use those too?

For our example let's assume the following: You've determined that the value of each new lead is $10 of profit, and you are generating paid leads that cost either $1, $5, or $9 each.

Which lead sources should you focus on?

The answer, of course, is all of them. Grab as many free leads as you can, and then go after the $1 leads, next the $5 leads, and so on.

I've heard many business owners online and offline brag that they don't advertise or market at all because they don't have to. When I hear that I know that the business is stuck at a level well below where it could and should be.

# CHAPTER 24

# DRAW YOUR IDEAL CLIENTS IF YOU WANT TO MEET THEM

**I**t took me a long time to realize who my most typical customer really is. I could have learned it a whole lot sooner and earned a lot more money had I conducted a simple survey among some of my most loyal customers. I didn't, however, and as a result I missed out on several early opportunities as my business grew.

While I won't share with you here exactly what my target prospect looks like, I can tell you that it is a very worthwhile exercise for you to draw your ideal target client or prospect on paper and then identify as many possible characteristics as possible. This will help you determine what content is needed to attract the members of our target audience.

I'm not forcing you to assume that your business only appeals to one type of person, but there almost certainly is an ideal customer that brings you most of your profits for the least amount of effort. These are the customers that just get it with you and you find them easy to please. They might even be the clients you take for granted. It's the sort of customer that you find yourself wishing you had more of, and not the sort of customer you find yourself wishing you had less of. It's the Pareto principle, or the "80/20 rule" at work. In this case 80 percent of your profits come from 20 percent of your customers.

Once you know the basic demographic information, preferences, age, income, education, and possibly gender or other differentiating qualities of your target prospects, then you will find it much easier to target your efforts towards obtaining more clients just like them as you create quality content and products for that audience.

I even suggest that you take some time to physically draw the persona of your target client. Give them a face. If you aren't a talented artist, find someone with some artistic skills and have them create this persona on paper for you. Your business may appeal to several different personas, but narrow it down to the most ideal prospects if at all possible. I help you identify and create mutually beneficial relationships with a different kind of ideal client in Chapter 87.

There are numerous ways to take advantage of having completed this process, not the least of which is to connect personally with several of your bulls-eye clients and find out what is working best for them and what they don't like about your business. The insight and focus you will gain will be powerful.

Each time I conducted this exercise either in my own business or with someone else's, I've discovered surprises. Odds are your business is more appealing than you realize to certain personas, and less appealing than you assumed to others. This does not mean you should change your personality, because that is impossible. Instead, use this information to go after your target prospects with intentionality.

Completing this exercise will also allow you to identify mutually beneficial partnership arrangements that can be pursued. Who else is going after a similar persona?

# PART 6

# START HANGING OUT WHERE YOUR PROSPECTS HANG OUT

**B**y now you probably realize that just having a website isn't enough. You're going to need traffic. Some of the most consistent advice that I've given other online entrepreneurs over the years is to go to where the traffic already is instead of trying to start your online venture by building your own website.

In my opinion far too many entrepreneurs consider building a website as their first step towards success online. As an alternate approach I teach my students and clients to find the places online where their target audience (or prospects) are already gathering and then actively engage with them in some fashion. Building a website comes much later, or possibly never.

For many entrepreneurs this means they should be finding other popular websites and then finding creative ways to serve their target audience or find ways to partner with the owner of the popular site.

In other sections of this book I've written about how I've used e-mail marketing to grow a large, loyal audience and I haven't needed any fancy websites in order to accomplish this. Instead I've gone to other online experts and popular websites and found ways to creatively partner with them in order to grow my own audience. Once I have an audience I can then determine what needs they have through a simple survey. In some cases a website was necessary in order to accommodate the needs of my audience, and only *then* was a website built.

# CHAPTER 25

# USING EBAY TO FIND YOUR AUDIENCE

**I** mentioned in a previous chapter that eBay can be a fantastic place for you to find prospects and eager fans for your product or even some services. Not all products are a good fit for eBay, but it's worth a shot for any business to try. Here's a recent success story from one of my students that is now running a successful Volkswagen Bug customization business:

> I gotta give you credit for my story, Jim. You are the one who showed me eBay and how to harness it by driving traffic to my site. My efforts have now spurred a great cult following of my business. My thanks to you.
>
> My Story:
> I was an indie filmmaker; since I was a small kid it was my dream to see my work up on the big screen. I wrote, directed, edited, and produced 10 films all on my own. I did them all on my own because I just did not have the $$ to hire people, so I made them dirt-cheap.
> I got into the Tribeca Film Festival, won numerous awards, and even had a feature action film go international. All was great! But there was no income really; I worked odd jobs to make a buck. My late twenties hit and I said I needed to make some money. I couldn't keep bumming off my folks. But I did not want to work for anyone else either. I knew I had the talents and the skills to do my own thing.
> My idea:
> All through my college and filmmaking years I had a classic Volkswagen (VW), but I knew nothing about other cars. I only knew the Bug. I am an artist so ya gotta have a Bug. I grabbed a 1968 Beetle that was

rotted to hell for $350 and I wanted to restore it. My father thought I was crazy but we did it together. I knew nothing about restoring cars; my dad had some mechanical skills because when he was young he worked in a Brooklyn garage, but **we had never worked on a VW**.

Thanks to the Internet, there are many resources to learn any craft you want. If you have the drive and a desire to do something great and be independent, there's never been a better time to be alive than now!

I learned these skills from you Mr. Cockrum, and sold that Bugger on eBay motors! We made food money on it! My father and I looked at each other and said, "We gotta get into this!" So from a one-car garage to now a 2000-square-foot facility, we are kicking butt! We developed a nice track record on eBay and **we are now taking orders for my "Build-A-Bug" program**. We are running our business with a year-and-a-half wait time. People want us to build a Bug just for them!

What made me stand out from the crowd is that I used my filmmaking skills to shoot my Bugs with music, titles, FX, you name it. No one is doing what I am doing when it comes to selling on eBay motors. All bidders are exposed to over 50 pictures of my cars and full high-definition video.

I also do "How To" Tips on Beetle restoration uploaded to YouTube (my ID on YouTube.com is brighteyefilms). These tip videos led me to sell a full two-hour DVD on Headliner installation (I sell the DVD using Kunaki.com, like you showed me). I answer two hours of fan mail in the morning and two hours at night just for the Bug biz.

Sorry this is so long-winded, but my example shows if you have a passion to be successful with a product you love, you can do it.

Every resource is available out there for you. I am always learning and staying up-to-date with the trends; doing this will give you an edge and make you stand out from your competition.

Chris Vallone
ClassicVWbugs.com

Another inspirational example of how eBay can be used to establish an eager audience is found in the strategy pursued by my student Nancy Alexander of LadybugWreaths.net.

When I first met Nancy she was selling her handmade wreaths one at a time on eBay for a decent price, but after some coaching she grew her business to include teaching others how to build wreaths. Her loyal following of "crafty" women now rely on her for the latest decorating and craft-making tips and strategies. She has the e-mail addresses of hundreds of customers, even more fans, and a very nice income as a result of her ongoing efforts.

This is also another great example of how giving away your secrets can lead to great things. This concept was one of the irrational habits I wrote about in Chapter 6. Nancy was hesitant at first when I suggested she should show others how to build wreaths the way she did. Her hesitance was understandable because she was making $60 to $80 for each wreath she sold on eBay, but in the end my advice made total sense to her because the profit margins on information products and the loyal following that she was able to build made it all more than worthwhile. It also takes a lot less work to ship out copies of DVDs than it does to build wreaths one at a time! This was a blessing to Nancy because of her long-term struggle with fibromyalgia. To read Nancy's inspirational story, visit her website at LadyBugWreaths.net.

If you missed it, go back and read the example I gave in Chapter 6 (Irrational Habit 1), where a doll-clothing maker decided to start growing her audience on eBay and now has a virtual empire as a result.

eBay is where millions of prospects and consumers browse every day for virtually every product imaginable. I've built much of my reputation on educating small businesses and online entrepreneurs on the little-known opportunities that exist on eBay under the radar. Rather than looking at eBay as simply a website where you can sell one item at a time to one customer at a time, I encourage you to see eBay as a source of dozens or hundreds of new leads weekly, even if you are only selling a handful of items at a time.

In its prime eBay was a phenomenal source of leads for thousands of businesses. The rules have changed a bit, but the opportunity is still there for businesses willing to take a creative look at the opportunity.

As eBay grew they began to implement rules to try to keep traffic from flowing off eBay. You'll need to be aware of eBay's link policies when trying to use their site as a marketing tool. For example, you can't blatantly link from an auction listing on eBay to one of your websites. You can, however, use a creative e-mail address in your auction listing in order to bring attention to the fact that you have a website that your shoppers might want to investigate. For example, if you sell outdoor gear on eBay and you also have an outdoor gear related website, then you can include the e-mail address such as "support@AlsOutdoorGear.com" inside each of your eBay auction listings. Savvy shoppers will notice the domain name hidden in your e-mail address and will likely stop by and check out your website.

Many of my most successful students and clients are using eBay in creative ways to generate leads. As long as you pay attention to the rules, there are many ways to get creative with your account.

Classified ads on eBay are also another opportunity worth investigating. The rules for classified ads on eBay are a little more lenient, and there is even more opportunity for you to generate good leads. When I speak of eBay classified ads, keep in mind that I'm not talking about the local classified ads service found at eBayclassifieds.com. I've not yet found a good use for that site. Instead I'm talking about the classified ads that appear on eBay.com right alongside all of the other auction listings. When setting up a new listing on eBay (in some countries, including the United States), there is an option to set up a classified ad instead of an auction or Buy It Now listing.

I've met very few fellow classified ads users on eBay, but there are some very creative marketers generating highly qualified leads every day as a result of their understanding of the classified ads opportunity that exists on eBay. Currently I have a popular video on YouTube that discusses more about classified ads on eBay and how they can be used creatively to generate leads. Just search for the term "eBay Classified Ads" and look for the video by SilentJimDotCom (that's my YouTube.com account name).

While not every business can generate leads using eBay, it is certainly easy to find out if it will work for you with just a little bit of experimentation.

# CHAPTER 26

# FIND GOOD MARKETING PARTNER SITES

For many businesses the customer base is already hanging out online on blogs, websites, and discussion forums related to its target niche market.

A quick search on the major search engines for each of the best keywords associated with your niche will produce several pages of potential partners. Each of these sites are potential partners for you to work with. These websites are the places where your future customers are already hanging out.

You'll find several other websites to add to your targeted list of potential partners if you add the word "blog" or the word "forum" to each of your Google, Bing.com, or Yahoo.com search queries.

Once you have your list, it's time to start forming relationships with each of the targeted sites. Even if you only wind up working with one or two of the fifty sites you find, it will have been well worth the effort.

In some cases your only option to gain exposure on these target sites will be to purchase advertising, but in almost all cases there are other creative possibilities available to you. Begin an intentional campaign of attracting the attention of the key decision makers on these sites by contributing to their success and by expressing your desire to partner up. Here are some creative ideas to try:

- Try to identify the people behind the website. You need to know who the key players are so that you can form real relationships with them.
- Make useful comments on blog posts or articles on their site or where you find things written about their site elsewhere online.
- Send them links to useful content that may be of interest to them (Google Alerts are great for tracking this, or to track bigger news trends around any given niche or topic use newstimeline.Googlelabs.com).

- Follow the website and, more important, the individual key players that run the site. Follow them on Twitter, Facebook, or YouTube and make supportive and relevant comments on the content they post there.
- Get their physical mailing address and send a creative card or gift expressing your appreciation and admiration for what they've done. Don't have an agenda when you reach out—just form a real relationship and give honest feedback.
- Send them great original articles that they can use as content. You don't have to ask permission first—just send it over!
- Find places online where the key players or the website itself is mentioned or discussed. Pay special attention to anyone that says something negative, and make a thoughtful reply defending the key players or the site. Trust me—they'll notice this. For example, a VP of PayPal called to thank me a couple of years ago after I spent some time defending PayPal on an open discussion forum. I had no agenda when writing my comments, but the VP went to great lengths to track me down so he could bounce some ideas off of me and then he sent me a T-shirt. It's good to have friends like that online.

Those types of strategies will help you to win over the key players and influencers at any website—even those big, cold sites that seem impossible to crack into. You'll slowly earn the right to partner with them in creative ways that others don't have access to.

Finding creative ways to create three-way wins is your next step. Check out Chapters 66 and 67 for more details on that concept.

# PART 7

# GET CREATIVE WITH THE MEDIA

**I** may not make any new friends in the world of mass media by saying this, but to me it seems that the traditional press is quickly losing most of its influence and power. (Can I get a witness?)

This isn't a shocking statement really, is it? That being said, there are still plenty of opportunities for great exposure using traditional media outlets.

Don't write off traditional media. Be ready for them when they come knocking, and learn to pursue them the right way.

# CHAPTER 27

# HAVE A PRESS KIT READY ON DEMAND

**T**raditional media outlets, such as newspapers or radio, sometimes still operate under the old rules. They like to see a Press Kit or Media Kit on your blog or website. If you don't have one they might move on to find a different expert or business that meets their needs. While there are various opinions as to what should go in such a kit, several basics are consistent.

- A basic bio about the key players, and a summary of your business, its products, and achievements. Attach a quality headshot of all key players in high-res format.
- A list of "as seen on" logos and names.
- Sample interview questions they should ask you.
- A list of your best testimonials.
- Copies of any articles or TV spots you've appeared in.
- A fact sheet listing out important dates, products, events, and so on. This includes date founded, dates of major product releases, dates of gatherings or seminars, and so on.
- Photos of everything that they can use, if necessary.
- Sample YouTube videos.
- Your story. Don't tell them the features of your product. Give them the story they need.
- Basic contact info for every key contact in your organization.

All of this information can be downloadable, but it may be smart to have hard copies of everything as well.

You don't have to have everything listed here, and you might add more of course, but the more prepared you are the easier it is for them to do their job. Traditional media is always working against a deadline, so they like to use sources that are responsive and all laid-out, ready to go.

# CHAPTER 28

# INFLUENCE THE INFLUENTIAL

**R**ather than attempt to establish a relationship with a media outlet in general, you should instead pursue relationships with the key reporters and writers that are a part of that media organization. Once you've identified the key players that you would love to be interviewed by, start stalking them in a friendly, useful way. Follow them on Twitter, Facebook, and so on and contribute to the discussions they seem to care most about. Find things that you have in common with them and strike up conversations on those topics.

## TIP

Once you've found a few influencers in your niche and begun following them on Twitter, use Google's free tool at followfinder.Googlelabs.com to locate several other similar experts and begin following them as well. Following someone on Twitter is a great way to start or form a relationship with them.

Use the same strategies that I discuss in Chapter 26 to build a relationship with reporters and influencers inside of any media organization. If you can form a relationship you'll be much more likely to be on their short list of experts that they will turn to when it comes time for interviews or articles related to your niche.

They'll also be far more likely to pay attention to the press releases you send them!

# CHAPTER 29

# PRESS RELEASE MARKETING

This is one of those chapters where I will really enjoy hearing from my readers about how they've applied these concepts in the past. If you've had some degree of success using press releases in creative ways in your business, please visit the resource page for this book (101FreeMarketing.com) and contribute your ideas to the conversation. By checking out the resource page for this book you'll also see the creative ideas that others have left.

While I haven't used press releases very often myself in my own business, I can tell you that even a press release that is completely ignored by major media outlets can still be a great source of traffic and back links for your website. This is because press releases that are submitted online are often archived and then posted permanently on major search engines. Depending on which press release service you use, this could generate a very high quality back link for your website. You should pay special attention to the keywords that you use in your article so that the search engines can detect and reward you for the content.

Also pay special attention to the title that you choose for your press release. Remember, a press release is a news story, it's not a sales pitch. For this reason the first paragraph of your press release needs to answer the major questions that every reporter is expecting to see. Answer the who, what, when, where, and why questions first. The rest of your press release is spent backing up the facts and claims that you make in your initial statements.

It should come as no surprise that most of the world isn't nearly as excited as you are about the latest news coming from your company. In order to create a better story for public consumption you should consider tying your press releases to a current trend in the general news media. Expand your circle of expertise to include bigger niche trends. This is one time when it pays to be more general instead of more specific in your niche expertise.

For example, if your company sells a specific kind of dog collar you are far more likely to have a press release get picked up by a major outlet if your topic is a general interest story involving recent dog care trends rather than a story about your new color options for collars. You get the idea.

Here are several of the most popular press release submission sites:

BusinessWire.com
GlobeNewsWire.com
MarketWire.com
Prnewswire.com
Prweb.com

# PART 8

# SMARTPHONES ARE TAKING OVER THE WORLD

**C**ell phones have become the equivalent of powerful minicomputers in the pockets of billions of people around the world. Cell phones now outnumber computers in total count, as well as time spent using the device.

While most cell users still don't have a smartphone, the trend is clearly heading in that direction.

Consumers are having what amounts to a love affair with their mobile phones. The evidence is all around us, and the numbers all back it up. While the number of desktop/laptop computer users is starting to level off, the number of mobile users has already bypassed the number of desktops and is continually rocketing upward. I could cite numerous studies to back up this claim, but 10 minutes of Google research will show the evidence of my claims in abundance.

It's almost as if the Internet is pushing a giant reset button and everything has to work on a small screen now. Call me crazy, but I'll sound like a genius if you pick this book back up in two years and re-read that sentence.

As in most other modern forms of marketing, the most effective strategies long term will be the low cost and free authentic strategies.

**Before I go any further talking about cell phones, though, here are some basic big picture tips:**
- Make sure that your website looks good on a small cell phone screen. A good mobile programming expert can convert any website into a

mobile friendly version that will appear when your site is pulled up on a mobile phone. If you happen to have a WordPress site as your website, a plug-in called WP–Touch is a great simple solution.

- Success with mobile marketing is not about getting mobile phone numbers from strangers. Never buy lists of numbers, and never collect them in creative ways that trick the owner of the number because it will certainly back fire. You want to have a friendly opt-in system and then send your followers only the relevant useful messages that they've agreed to get. Unlike e-mail spam, text spam costs your followers real money to receive in many cases, so the level of potential anger is far greater.

- While smartphones and text-enabled phones are becoming more popular all the time, not everyone has one yet. Keep in mind that you will be leaving some people out entirely when you engage in this form of marketing.

# CHAPTER 30

# TEXT MARKETING CAN'T BE IGNORED

**T**ext messaging doesn't require you or your customer to have a website, a smartphone, or even Internet access, and it has more than a 90 percent read rate.

Proceed with caution though.

Rule 1 with text messaging is: Send only what prospects and customers *want* to get.

Text messages are far more likely to be read, and get read far more often than any other form of marketing that is discussed in this book (for example, e-mail, Facebook, Twitter, and so on).

If you can give your customers an incentive to opt-in to your valuable text message campaign, you can begin enjoying one of the highest response rates for marketing that is currently available. Use texting for automatic reminders, coupons, special event announcements, and so on. I am aware of several emerging services and technologies that are aimed at helping you tap into the full potential of the text marketing opportunity, but I'm hesitant to put these into the book because several of them are such new services that I want to let them prove themselves first. The book resource page will have the most recent recommendations and suggestions that I find in the cell phone text-marketing arena. Come share with us what you are finding as well!

## TEXT MESSAGES SELL PIZZA?

As I was in the middle of writing this very chapter I was contacted by a student of mine named George. He had found himself let go recently from a corporate position he'd held with a cellular company, and was so willing to do anything for income that he found himself back delivering pizza for a well known U.S.-based chain pizza shop. As a father of three with a young wife, this was obviously less than ideal.

As a member of OfflineBiz.com (where we teach online marketers how to apply their skills to real world businesses), George had learned recently about a tool that allowed businesses to form strong relationships with their current customer base by using the power of text messaging. George convinced his manager to start a flyer campaign promoting a free giveaway contest that would, hopefully, ignite a large following of fans and subscribers to their texting campaign. Within a few weeks they had grown a list of 600 local customers with all their contact info (including cell phone numbers), so that they could then offer pizza specials instantly at any time via text messaging.

As soon as they had 300 opt-in phone numbers they ran a test— rather, they had to run a test. The pizza shop had over-ordered dough and was due to dispose of a whole lot of it the next day if it wasn't used immediately. Unfortunately, it was the slowest day of the week for them as well, so they weren't too sure what to expect, nor were they optimistic.

They sent out a special offer to the 300 cell phones that they had numbers for, using text messaging, and received an extra *80 pizza orders, virtually instantly.* This was the first time they had tried out their list and it worked! Within a few days the list was up to 600, and it's still growing steadily.

George now has the pizza chain regionally, and perhaps even nationally, looking at him as a big answer to their marketing needs. There are also multiple other businesses (or as George says, a "laundry list") looking to George and his new marketing company because of George's ability to grasp the power of opt-in text marketing.

To hear the actual, 100 percent unplanned phone call that George made to me (I asked him if I could record it because he was so excited in the e-mail he sent me), please visit the 101FreeMarketing.com page and look for the "Text Message Marketing" resources.

# INCH-WIDE, MILE-DEEP MARKETING

**W**ith Part 9 we begin the second phase of this book, as we transition into strategies for building your influence and developing true trust among your customers and prospects.

This is made possible by the global networks that connect us all in ways we don't even understand fully yet.

Never before have tiny niche market ideas had so much opportunity for so much attention globally. Even the smallest local businesses and content creators have the chance to benefit from exposure well outside their geographical region.

It's time for you to be a leader.

Every imaginable hobby, interest, passion, or product that has more than a handful of global fans now needs a leader. This is your chance to become a world's foremost expert. The narrower your focus, the better. It's time to think inch wide and mile deep as you gather fans.

Even if your business is setting up food stands at fairs and flea markets, you could become world famous for it if you do it right. Why not develop a course that teaches other less experienced food vendors (or those looking to get into the business) how to do it right? There is a worldwide audience potentially! Sell the course on eBay and grow a following.

Sound ridiculous?

Others are doing it right now. There is a guy on eBay that's been doing exactly that for several years now, selling a good number of his courses every week. He decided not to settle for being the owner of a food cart business. He's now (or easily could call himself) an expert in the niche with hundreds of customers listening to his advice.

If you can provide first-class information at a low cost or for free and grab the attention of your audience with a potent message, then you can earn their trust.

Want some examples from my businesses?

**Here are some of the niche arenas that I work in:**
- "Internet Consulting Expert for Brick-and-Mortar Businesses": I help Internet Marketers learn to apply their marketing skills to real-world businesses that desperately need the help. This skill lead to the launching of OfflineBiz.com.
- "Multiple Creative Income Streams Expert": Teaching stay-at-home parents and entrepreneurs multiple income stream strategies (MySilentTeam.com & JimCockrum.com).
- "Emerging Media Marketing Expert": I can show any organization or individual how to grow a loyal following for nearly any cause or product using e-mail and social media marketing (ListBuildingClass.com).
- "Creative eBay Marketer": I can teach you to use eBay and other online selling forums as a steady, autopilot source of lifelong repeat customers (SilentSalesMachine.com).
- "Internet Entrepreneur Advisor": Creating and sharing tools and ideas that simplify the process of succeeding in Internet business.

While these niche markets are all related, I haven't found it necessary to limit myself to just one area of expertise. The only limiting factors are your time, commitment, and vision.

As I create quality content and attract loyal followers in each of these areas, my influence will continue to increase. The supporting evidence of my "world's foremost expert" title continues to mount for me, as it can for you, as I explain in the next chapter.

# CHAPTER 33

# BECOME A WORLD'S FOREMOST EXPERT—FAST

I first got the advice to start calling myself a "world's foremost expert" from Paul Hartunian. At the time he was calling himself a foremost expert on dating and relationships. According to Paul, the power of the title alone was much of what propelled him to success in this crowded niche. He wasn't worried about being challenged by other experts either. He just set about creating quality content that solidified the title in the minds of his followers.

There is great power in a title, even if it's a title you give yourself. The world is looking online for experts and the simple decision to start calling yourself one will open doors that otherwise would never have been opened, even if your expertise is in a small niche.

For example, I've been approached on multiple occasions to do radio and newspaper interviews simply because my name appears frequently online next to the words "online auction expert." Reporters will often type in a simple Google search in order to find the experts that they need for a story, and if the topic is "online auctions," or any of the other topics I've created content for, then the odds are my name will come up on their radar. If I'm bold enough to call myself an expert they always believe me and I've never been challenged.

Start creating content online related to your inch-wide, mile-deep niche and confidently call yourself a foremost expert as you do it. The world is longing for leaders. Just make sure to back up your claim with a lot of quality content.

Here's a recent story that a newsletter reader of mine sent me that shows how he confidently built a large global following around his relatively small niche expertise.

# PUT YOUR EXPERTISE TO USE!

"I had 10 years experience running a martial arts school. I started the school from scratch with no credit, no education, and no money—and then I grew it successfully to roughly 200 students. I felt I had a lot to say about the martial arts industry that just wasn't being said in the mainstream publications.

So I wrote a book.

I wasn't willing to settle for getting a few dollars off of each book sale, so I aimed higher.

That's when I started seriously studying how to market products and information online. I encountered a pretty steep learning curve at first, but within a few short years I had overcome any initial challenges and my book had garnered a die-hard underground cult following. I managed this with little, if any, mainstream press coverage, and well before social media had become a factor in viral marketing. Mostly, I relied on organic search engine traffic and word-of-mouth as well as some pay-per-click ads.

It's encouraging to know that countless martial arts instructors who followed my book to success are now running successful schools. Without a doubt, that's the most rewarding thing about marketing my ideas as an expert.

And honestly, without folks like Jim Cockrum freely sharing their knowledge and experience about Internet marketing online, I'd never have been able to learn the ins and outs of online marketing. Thanks Jim, and thanks to all the other Internet marketing coaches who helped me along the way, and who are too numerous to mention here."

Mike Massie
Small-dojo-big-profits.com

Some stats about Mike's info business: He has about 2,200 loyal e-mail newsletter sub-scribers and over 100 studio owners paying him monthly to be part of his membership site. He estimates that he's sold over 3,000 self-published reports, books, audios, and manuals and he is a paid coach for multiple studio owners who rely on his advice.

# CHAPTER 34

# FIND FORUM FAME

One of the best ways to establish yourself as an expert in any market is to seek out and begin participating in the most active forums that are being used by members of your target audience. You won't find success in a discussion forum if you are constantly trying to sell something though. Your credibility is established instead by being helpful, available, and thorough in the replies and assistance that you offer other forum members.

Consider the success that my clients Steven Sashen and his wife, Lena, have had with only basic forum participation as the core of their marketing efforts.

Here's their story.

"We brought online marketing to the Stone Age.

We launched a website at InvisibleShoe.com selling "barefoot" sandals. It's a modern take on a 10,000-year-old idea.

Currently, we are selling over 400 pairs of Invisible Shoes every month, grossing over $15,000, and still growing. We're about to launch four new products (that our customers have been begging for), so we expect those numbers to increase dramatically in the next couple months, even though we'll be selling sandals in the winter.

We've also had 50 retailers sign-up to carry our products (and our plan is to get over 500 in our first year with a retail product).

We made our first sale 16 hours after we launched the site.

My wife and I quit our day jobs three months later.

Now we're working with a group of consultants who helped build Reebok from less than $1,000,000 to over $1,000,000,000, and we are on track to be an eight-figure business by this time next year.

A lot of the promotional tactics we learned at OfflineBiz.com have been relevant for our non-local business. Hearing Jim extol the value of submitting to the video sites was an inspiration to make a lot of videos and we are gearing up to make even more.

**The two biggest things we did to promote the site were:**

1. Participating on forums where people were already talking about barefoot running. We didn't pitch our product. We just joined in on the conversation and had a simple signature file at the end of each post that let people know we had free do-it-yourself videos on our website.

2. Sharing how-to videos on YouTube and other video sites where I showed how to make our product without ever buying our product! I gave complete plans to do it yourself with items you might have around the house.

**The lessons:**

One of the things that I've found is that people respond to people. That is, the more you (and your employees) can be visible, accessible, and available online, the more your potential customers can relate to you. And the more they relate to you (or, again, the people in your company), the more connected to you and your products they feel. And the more connected they feel, the more they want to do business with you. You can't make this a strategy; you simply have to do it honestly.

Don't be afraid to giveaway a lot of free information—I've had dozens of runners come up to me at races and show me the shoes they've made following my instructions. While they didn't buy anything from me, they've referred others who have. And, maybe, some day, I'll offer something they can't make on their own and they'll become customers (actually, it's guaranteed that I'll have that product to offer them)."

Steven Sashen
InvisibleShoe.com

I can't even begin to recall the large number of success stories that I've encountered in the last decade that all began the same way. So many successful entrepreneurs have either started out or have expanded their current business in great ways simply by hanging out on discussion forums among people that are like-minded. By doing this and by providing useful assistance to as many people as you can, you'll soon notice trends and needs among your fellow forum participants. Inevitably there will be a need that you can meet and begin to profit from while working with the very people that you have the most in common with.

# PART 10

# VIDEO IS NO
# LONGER OPTIONAL

The increasing popularity of Internet-based video is undeniable. Video is quickly becoming a basic necessity of being taken seriously online. The viral power of video is well documented, and if you aren't in the game you are missing out. It costs virtually nothing to get into the game.

One of the key common elements that you'll notice among nearly all online success stories is the use of video in one fashion or another. This is a trend that isn't likely to change anytime soon. If you want to be taken seriously, get used to the idea of creating useful video content for your prospects and followers.

# CHAPTER 35

# MAKE YOUR VIDEOS GO VIRAL

**B**y now you've likely heard the term "viral video." When a video begins to get a lot of attention and traction and is being passed around social networks it is said to have gone viral.

Of the tens of thousands of videos that are uploaded to YouTube.com daily, what is it about a handful of them that makes them go viral? Several people have attempted to identify a formula, or they have claimed to be able to make it happen repeatedly, but few have achieved any sort of predictable consistency. There are some common elements, though. These elements include videos that:

- Make people laugh
- Are cutting edge with their content or delivery
- Surprise the audience
- Feature an uplifting message
- Are cute (kids, animals)
- Tell a compelling story
- Are short (less than two to three minutes)

While many of these factors can be fairly hard to achieve intentionally, you should constantly be alert and aware of events and circumstances around you that may lend themselves to being content in a viral video.

A more predictable strategy for gaining attention on YouTube.com is to focus on creating a consistent stream of useful content that includes a clear call to action (i.e., "Join our mailing list"). Even if only a handful of people ever see your video in the first year, there could easily come a time in the future where the subject matter of your video becomes fodder for a larger conversation and at that point it could get passed around virally. As long as the content of the video you create has some useful value, or is entertaining, then it is worth having been made.

**Reminders:**
- I wrote about creating lead capture and squeeze pages in Chapter 7. Directing your YouTube viewers to your lead capture page is a great way to get leads into your funnel.
- When naming your YouTube account use a creative name that represents your brand. In my case, I named one of my YouTube accounts "SilentJimDotCom." While I'm unsure how many visitors I get to my squeeze page as a result of this name choice, I'm sure that I pick up a few subscribers per week because of all the exposure.

## CHAPTER 36

# 24 MARKETING VIDEOS YOU SHOULD HAVE

**M**y friend and online video marketing expert, Mike Koenigs, has a proven formula that he calls the $10 \times 10 \times 4$ formula. The $10 \times 10 \times 4$ formula is a simple yet effective way to create a body of valuable video content that your prospects will go crazy for. At the same time it establishes you as a credible expert and as someone that can be trusted on any important topic.

**Here's how to do it, straight from Mike's own words:**
1. Write down the top 10 frequently asked questions about your product or service.
2. Write down the top 10 questions a potential buyer *should* be asking you about your product or service. These are the important things that differentiate you from your competitors.
3. Record 20 short videos responding to each question. Each video response should be 30 seconds to 3 minutes in length (30 to 90 minutes total). If you don't have a camera, you can make videos with PowerPoint and Camtasia, or Keynote and ScreenFlow if you have a Mac.
4. Record four short mini-videos (three minutes each).
   a. "To Get More, Go Here" Video. At the end of each video, you tell people where to go to get all 19 videos. This is an offer to take them from your video to a Video Lead Page (explained below).
   b. "Enter your name and e-mail to get all 20 videos." Put this on your Video Lead Page. It's your chance to connect with the visitor and explain your offer and why they should sign up.

   **c.** "Thank You for Signing Up" Video. Put this on your "Thank You" page —so when someone fills in the form, you tell them they'll receive their video as soon as they click a confirmation link that your autoresponder e-mails to them.

   **d.** "Buy My Stuff Video." You'll put this on your website and your outbound e-mails.

5. Once you've completed these videos make a lead capture page or squeeze page. This is where you're going to send people after they watch your videos.

6. Upload your videos to as many video sharing, social bookmarking, podcast directories, social networks, and blogs as possible. It will take a couple of days to do this manually.

For more information about Mike's content distribution systems please visit the resource page (www.101FreeMarketing.com).

# CHAPTER 37

# ESSENTIAL VIDEO MARKETING TOOLS

T he tools and software that make using video increasingly simple will undoubtedly continue to get better. As of this writing I have some favorites, but as with all technology these recommendations could be very out of date within a short time. The resource page of this book will contain up-to-date links and advice as well, to help you make video as simple and as effective as possible.

**Some basic tools to help you get started with online video:**
- Kodak Zi8 camera or a Flip video camera (or your cell phone).
- The Kodak Zi8 is currently one of my favorites. It's one of those tiny video cameras with the added benefit of an external mic jack that creates great audio. I recently won a couple of these and I can say they are fantastic. My kids are taking great videos and posting them easily to YouTube (my 10-year-old has it down). The price is coming down on all-powerful video equipment, and even cell phones are becoming capable of capturing good videos.
- Sony Vegas Software. This software is currently the standard for video editing for many online marketers. Find a teenager to do the editing for you . . . they know how to do this stuff.
- YouTube, Viddler, EZS3.com, and Easy Video Player.
- The sites YouTube, Viddler, and Vimeo are all options for hosting and playing your videos. These are public access services where random viewers are likely to stumble upon your content.
- For larger videos, many marketers (including me) are starting to use EZS3.com's service. Use their video player tools to put nice borders and play buttons on your videos and host them on any of your sites.

This is the service I used for my ListBuildingClass.com content, which is a course that has content delivered 100 percent online to students that take it.

- Camtasia, OpenOffice, Gmail.
- A powerful way to present a video is in a PowerPoint format with a voiceover. Make it fast paced—don't just read what's on the screen. You can easily create these types of videos by using screen capture software such as Camtasia. Most of the screen capture videos that I make and upload are done with Camtasia on a PC. The Macintosh version of Camtasia isn't nearly as good, but on a PC I love it. The only reason I keep a PC in my office is to make my Camtasia screen capture videos. My YouTube.com account is full of them. Check out SilentJimDotCom on YouTube to see some of them. Screen capture and presentation-style video is great if you aren't quite comfortable appearing on camera just yet.
- To make a PowerPoint-style slide show you can use PowerPoint (expensive), or check out the presentation software on OpenOffice.org, or even Google documents (which comes free with a Gmail account). Both do a great job for me and neither will cost you a penny.
- Want to get your confidence up about online video? How about creating a super cool slide show of digital images in about five minutes flat. If you can use e-mail and know how to attach a picture to an e-mail message, then you have all the skills that you'll need to handle animoto.com. I promise that you'll be blown away by what you can create just by uploading a few photos and then clicking the create button. It's that simple.

**The bottom line is this:**

Experts make videos. If you want to be perceived as an expert, you need to make videos and get them out there.

# CHAPTER 38

# Make Video Even If You Have a Face for Radio

You don't have to spend very much time on YouTube.com to discover that it's not just the pretty and articulate people with nice editing skills that are making videos. If you are going to achieve expert status online then you'll need to get over whatever fears you have of making and using online video. Remember, it actually works against you to try to be too slick and too polished when presenting your ideas using online video. More than ever before prospects appreciate online experts that are real and that deliver useful content regardless of how slick the presentation is. This isn't to say that you should ignore quality altogether when producing video, but you should never be discouraged from putting up content that you are worried is less than perfect.

I realize that some people are very shy about appearing on camera. If that's you, I have some good news. It doesn't have to be your face or your voice featured in the video content that you create. Your viewers are much more interested in the content of the video than in the details of whose face and whose voice is appearing. Many of my most effective videos contain no face time at all, but instead show the viewers screenshots of different websites and online tools that I'm demonstrating. When creating online tutorial-type videos I use Camtasia software to capture and record both the contents of the website that I'm viewing as well as my own voiceover commentary.

A great example of the power of online video can be found in the story of Ted Williams. Ted was a homeless man in early 2011 until a caring passerby took the time to record Ted's incredible voice and posted the video to YouTube. Within two days the video had 5 million views and Ted had multiple high-profile job offers. By Ted's own admission he has only a face for radio, but the power of viral video gave him a new lease on life.

# PART 11

# DELIVER CURRENT CONTENT CONSTANTLY

**I**t's getting harder and harder to force your message into the lives of busy people that are already focused on other things that they care more about. It is increasingly simple for all of us to surround ourselves with *only* the content and messages that we wish to receive. We are almost insulted by anything else that forces itself into our attention.

Great content is not slick brochures and fancy videos touting all of the features of your latest and greatest products. Great content is simply defined by your prospects as, "exactly the right information at exactly the right time I need it." Ideally, it's also free to consume.

If you can find a way to position yourself as an expert that frequently delivers great content, you won't be able to contain the number of leads and prospects that will beat a path to your door.

# CHAPTER 39

# CALL YOURSELF AN AUTHOR AND SELL MORE

**C**all yourself an author starting today.

If you've never called yourself an author before, I want you to add that title to your short list of comebacks when someone asks you what you do. The rest of this section is dedicated to convincing you why you should take this advice starting today, even if you don't have a book (yet) and even if you can't or don't want to write anything ever.

I think you'll discover, as I did, that by simply calling yourself an author great things will start to happen inside you and around you.

It may seem like I'm leaving out the fact that you don't have a book published (yet), but I address that in a moment. The benefits of actually having a book in print are well documented, and I discuss that later, but trust me, you *are* already an author, even if you don't have a book, and I can prove it to you in a moment.

Here's a brief history lesson that helps supports my vantage point on this subject. It's only in the past few decades that literacy has become common. History tells us that it used to be a *very* big deal to even have access to the required education to be able to read. Even having a book of any kind on hand was a big deal in the not-so-distant past. Literacy is now at an all time high globally in comparison. Being a reader is no longer considered an astonishing achievement, but rather a starting point. The same transition is starting to happen with the awe surrounding authors.

To be an author 150 years ago meant that you were a great writer, worthy of the rare and expensive resources required, including paper, ink, and the rarer-still resource of consumers called readers.

Thanks to technology and the Internet you no longer need paper, ink, or even readers in order to get your ideas out, but somehow all cultures still hold the title author (defined as "one who writes") in the highest esteem. Just as the esteem that came with literacy slowly vanished, so likely will the esteem associated with calling yourself an author, but for those of us paying attention we are well-positioned to take advantage of our justly earned title of author before the term becomes saturated within a decade or so.

You are probably an author without realizing it (and so are millions of fools, but let's not dwell on that too long for our purposes here). See Figure 39.1.

We are all authors now, since so much of what we think today we record and share instantly with others. We share ideas with the world easily on our blogs, in text messages, in online articles, on Facebook posts, on Twitter accounts, and on websites. If you have any of those things you are already an author according to any dictionary definition, and you should purposefully call yourself by the highly-esteemed title you've rightfully earned.

Sure, in the past the title author was reserved for someone that had unique skills with words and could craft them together masterfully to entertain or

**Figure 39.1**

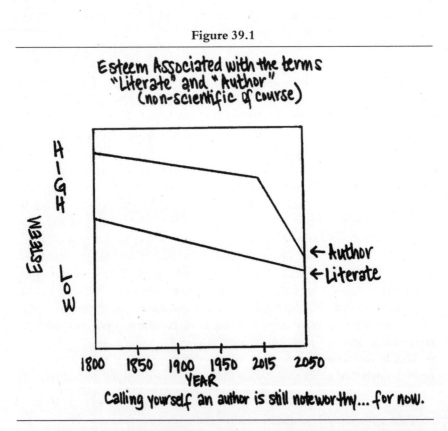

Esteem Associated with the terms
"Literate" and "Author"
(non-scientific of course)

← Author
← Literate

1800   1850   1900   1950   2015   2050
                    YEAR

Calling yourself an author is still noteworthy... for now.

educate. Authors had books inside a neatly contained volume on paper held together with glue and hard covers. Those skills may be just as rare today as they have ever been, but my theory still holds. We are all authors, just not necessarily great writers.

Thanks to the Internet age you don't even have to be a great writer in order to be a popular author. For proof of this just check out some of the most-read blogs of our time. Spelling, punctuation, sentence structure, and even slang are all mashed together in a way that would make your high school grammar teacher wince.

Here is why I chose to start calling myself an author: When I left the corporate world and began working full-time on the Internet I got a lot of questions from friends, family, and former colleagues. They'd ask me things like, "So what exactly is it you do now, Jim?"

I was unsure how to respond because my work consisted of a random mix of being an eBay seller, a website developer (a *bad* one), an online marketing enthusiast, an e-mail marketing specialist, a blogger, an affiliate marketer, an idea pioneer, a customer service representative for my own business, a business consultant for other people's businesses, and an overall content creator.

It was impossible to summarize it all for dinner conversations until I discovered the one word that cut through the maze for me.

Early on in my online entrepreneurial career I noticed something strange happened almost instantly when I began calling myself simply an author.

Suddenly I was more interesting and more listened to in business circles because I was instantly understood. Along with being more understood I was more confident and more respected. Suddenly I was treated like an expert, and good things came as a result.

I also felt the internal pressure to continue creating content worthy of my newly found title!

Suddenly radio hosts contacted me for interviews, magazines got my name from the web and asked me to do articles, the *Wall Street Journal* needed an author/expert for a column they were doing and they sought me out...all because I was an author—and I didn't even have a book on the shelf! All I had were a couple of eBooks that were selling as downloads.

> Do you remember the first time you put on reading glasses and looked at yourself in the mirror and thought, "Hey, these make me look smarter!" Calling yourself an author is sort of like that, only other people think it, too.

It's time to call yourself an author.

Never mind that you don't have a book out yet! Having a book is not a requirement for you to earn the title of author.

**You are an author if you:**
- Intend to write a book someday, and you've jotted some initial thoughts down on a napkin
- Have written a blog post
- Have spoken ideas into a recording device
- Have sent an educational or entertaining e-mail to more than one person and they WANTED to read it (that means you are a great author actually)
- Have a Twitter or Facebook account and people you don't know are now following you because of what you believe, say, or write
- Have an interesting story to tell, or an interesting perspective on any topic
- Know someone that meets one of the above qualifications and you are willing to write a book for them

If someone presses you for more information about what you've written, be prepared to give more detail, of course. A great answer though is simply, "I'm working on a book about (fill in the blank)."

Trust me, 90 percent of everyone that ever hears that sentence will make a mental note that you are now their instant expert on all things regarding your chosen topic of (fill in the blank).

An author is simply someone that has a story to tell or a unique perspective to share and is willing to put it out there. Are you willing? If so, call yourself an author and then read the next chapter to find out how easy it is to back it all up with something "written" and "published." I put written and published in quotes because writing is no longer required in order to get your message out, and neither is publishing.

Start calling yourself an author today and you'll be pleasantly amazed at what comes about directly as a result.

# CHAPTER 40

# WRITE A BOOK FOR AN INSTANT SALES BOOST

In the previous chapter I did my best to convince you that you need to begin calling yourself an author starting immediately. Now is probably a good time to talk about backing that up with an actual book.

Relax.

You don't have to be a great writer, or even like writing, to be a good or even great author.

The tools and technology that are available to us today make it easier than ever to accomplish the task of putting together quality content for easy distribution.

Specifically in this chapter I'd like to discuss how easy it is for you to put together a real book that can be given away, sold online via Amazon.com, and even be distributed widely on bookstore shelves.

Your best possible excuse at this point though is this:

"But Jim, isn't it true that most authors never make any serious money from their efforts?"

You got me there, sort of . . .

I know for a fact that nearly all authors that set out to become rich or famous by writing a book fail, probably more frequently than do the aspiring actors that move to Hollywood or musicians that moved to Nashville hoping to strike it big. While some do meet their goals, we know for a fact that the vast majority of them never do. I'm not talking about that sort of mindset for your book efforts though. Sure, you'll be making serious money, gaining great exposure, and expanding your influence, but it won't be just based on the volume of sales of your book. Even if your book only sells a small handful of copies it could still be a raging success for you.

Here are some examples where the sales numbers just don't matter.

At one of my membership websites we teach our Internet marketing enthusiast members how to effectively bring Internet marketing concepts to real-world businesses that just don't quite understand how to use the Internet yet as an effective marketing tool.

I frequently discourage members from passing out business cards to people they meet, and instead I encouraged them to pass out a small printed book (not a report mind you, but a book) that explains a few basic principles of Internet marketing.

For example: Let's pretend you are a pet store owner in Small Town, America. One day a polite young man walks into your store and says, "I know how to bring you more business using the Internet and I can prove it. Here is a book I wrote on the subject that I think will give you some great ideas. I'm a pet lover myself and I'd love to help you out. Please give this book a read if you don't mind, and then give me a call. If you aren't interested there is another pet store across town that I'll be going to in a couple days and I can only work with one of you." He then puts in your hand a very nice looking, off-the-shelf quality book titled *The Small Business Guide to Floods of Internet Business.*

Another example: You own a Martial Arts studio. A nice-looking book with a professional picture of you on the cover is given to each visiting family. The book is titled *The 10 Benefits of Martial Arts in Your Child's Life.* Think that might help business a little? Even if people don't crack the book open (most of them never will), it's still way better than a business card or a brochure, don't you think?

Or how about this: You are an aspiring engineer seeking a position with some of the most prominent companies in your industry. Would you rather have just a resume to hand your prospective employers, or a wow-factor package to put in their hands that includes a book that is all about the biggest trends in your industry? I'm talking about a real book with an ISBN number, bar code on the back, slick cover, and so on.

In each of these cases, if you are the one being handed the book, ask yourself these questions:

Would you be impressed?
Is a book better than a business card or resume in each case?
Are you likely to remember this person as an expert?

Another question: Is the goal of being a bestseller even on the radar in any of these examples? Of course it isn't, but the book is still a very powerful marketing tool, isn't it?

Let's write a book.

> Even if your book only sells a small handful of copies it could still be a raging success for you.

There are entire books written on the subject of how to write a book. If you are the cautionary type, perhaps you want to buy one of those books now that I've got you excited about the prospect of writing one of your own. If, however, you'd like to just get right down to it, then below you'll find some ideas that will get the ball rolling for you.

These suggestions are based only on my experience, but there is a degree of credibility behind them because I have sold a lot of my own writing, and I *don't really enjoy writing.*

Start with an outline. I'm not talking about the detailed sort of outline that we all had to do in high school before writing a report (I just got a shiver thinking about it). I'm talking about the sort of thing you might jot on a napkin. List the 10 concepts that you want to cover in your book.

Next, organize those concepts into some sort of order. Try to make it all flow chronologically, or logically.

Under each major point list a handful of sub-points and facts that will support what you have to say on the major topic. This is the hardest part of the book in my opinion.

If you don't mind writing, now is the time to start writing.

If you're opposed to writing, or if you're not very good at it, now is the time to get creative. You have several options at this point, thanks to technology.

**You could:**
- Hire a ghostwriter.
- Record yourself talking about each section of your book and then give those recordings to a transcription service such as internettranscribers.com (I love those guys).
- Buy voice-recording software, such as Dragon NaturallySpeaking (which I'm using right now by the way), and record yourself while the computer writes. It takes some getting used to, but if you are someone that tends to think in logical order, it will flow very easily. Keep in mind—there are people you can pay to edit your work! Just get the ideas down on paper (or into your computer).

You are going to need some cover art for your book, of course. Don't do this yourself, and don't have a friend do it. You want this done by a professional, and it's not difficult to pull it off. I suggest you use a service like 99Designs.com. You write out a description of what you'd like to see on your cover and submit it to 99Designs.com. Next, multiple artists and professionals will write up detailed proposals and show you simple graphics and pricing, hoping that you will accept their offer to do the cover work. You pick the work and the price that you like best, and once the work is completed to your satisfaction, you pay for the service.

*TIP:* You'll likely never be totally happy with the finished product. This is a lesson I've had to learn several times. No website, computer program, business idea, or book is ever truly complete, but if you wait until it feels perfect you'll miss the window of opportunity every time.

Next I suggest you look into a service like createspace.com (owned by Amazon.com), or Lulu.com to assist you in getting your book physically put together and published. There is no longer a need to print hundreds or thousands of books when you launch a new title. "Print on demand" has revolutionized the process of creating a book. You can have a few copies printed when you need them, and even have them shipped directly to your customers when they buy them online, without ever touching the books.

# CHAPTER 41

# WRITE AN E-BOOK IN DAYS AND BENEFIT FOR YEARS

**I**f the idea of having a real book is still a bit intimidating, or if you don't feel quite ready for it, consider the option of writing an e-book.

The e-books I write are simple PDF files that can be sent as an e-mail attachment, or downloaded and easily distributed instantly anywhere in the world where there is an Internet connection. I've sold tens of thousands of copies of e-books, so I'm well versed on the subject.

Writing your first e-book could be as simple as creating a 20-page document and then saving it as a PDF file. A PDF formatted file is preferred because it can be opened by anyone on any computer (Mac or PC).

My experience with e-books has been life-changing. I wrote my first 20-page, e-book over a decade ago and within just a few weeks my life began to change forever. I've talked at length about the power of a book, and even the power of calling yourself by the title of author, so I won't dwell on that any longer, but I can tell you that having e-books floating around the Internet has made me a lot of money.

For over 10 years now I've had the privilege of waking up each day, logging on to my computer, and checking the statistics of how many books I sold while I was sleeping. It's a feeling that never gets old. These books are delivered electronically as downloadable files to customers that purchase them from my various websites. The popularity of such downloadable products is booming.

One of the best ways to establish yourself as a credible thought leader in any niche market is to create an e-book product. Even if you simply record an interview with other experts in the niche, you will still be perceived as an expert for having completed a book project and the marketing potential is limitless.

An e-book should be a lead generating tool that gives away great content, while establishing your expertise. Don't make it a big sales pitch, and don't fill it with fluff content. The customers that buy or even download something for free are expecting a great first impression, so put great information inside. Selling information is the starting line for a life-long relationship (hopefully) with a new customer. It's not the finish line where I finally made some money. The customer needs to feel like they got 10 times the value from the purchase or I've failed them.

For a good example of just how much work can and should go into making a great e-book offer (even one you giveaway), check out "Irrational Habit 4" in Chapter 6.

Some thoughts from an e-book veteran:

*You can't have a protect-my-ideas mindset because it works against you.*

There is a mentality you'll have to adapt if you're going to be successful as an e-book author. The reality is, your product will be passed around to people who haven't paid for it (if it's any good at all). Just plan on that happening and use it to your advantage. Whenever I create content that I know will be going into an e-book (or anywhere online for that matter), I intentionally include multiple links, references, and stories that all lead the reader back to my websites, blogs, mailing lists, and so on. By doing this I'm actually ensuring that even the most blatant of copyright violations against my material will actually be a huge marketing boost for my overall business. This is one of the most common concerns that I hear when working with new e-book authors, but once you have the correct mindset you'll quickly realize that it's a non-issue. I actually enjoy seeing my e-book products being secretly distributed on piracy download websites. It's all free marketing from my vantage point.

My colleague Jeremy Schoemaker calls it having "a plan for piracy." I liked that term so much that I asked his permission to use it in this book. Back when cell ringtones were a huge phenomenon, Jeremy began giving away and selling ringtones along with instructions on how to install them. It wasn't long, however, before pirates began illegally distributing his ringtones and instructions from their own websites. Rather than chase the pirates down one by one, Jeremy simply included instructions on how users might make a small donation to him as part of his installation instructions. The pirates helped him spread the word, and Jeremy quickly banked $15,000 he otherwise never would have had because of the efforts of those violating his copyright.

**I'm obviously all for spreading my content around, but there are times when catching the bad guy in the act is nice. Here are a couple of options:**

- Copyscape (www.copyscape.com). Allows you to enter a few lines of text from your copy and instantly find out if others have copied your content and posted it online.
- Switchblade (http://www.documentsecurityalliance.com and digitalwatermarkingalliance.com both offer several options for securing and protecting your content and images).

## HOW WILL YOU CREATE AND DISTRIBUTE YOUR E-BOOK?

The same resources and processes that I showed you in the previous chapter regarding getting a real book completed apply here as well. Even the process of putting together a professional cover for your finished product is about the same—only this time you don't need camera-ready art. A nice looking e-book image will do. The only difference is, you're going to need a website to sell or giveaway your e-book product from. This could be your blog, or a one-page sales page site, designed specifically to tell visitors about the content of your book and encourage them to purchase it. You'll find many great examples of this at Clickbank.com—a service used by many e-book authors.

I started using Clickbank.com 10 years ago when they were a small company with a handful of employees. They have now gone on to become the most popular and effective way to sell information products online and employ a rather large staff. They handle multiple millions of dollars of transactions weekly. Clickbank.com specializes in helping e-book authors and digital content creators with the sales part of their business. They handle the transaction by billing the customer, making sure the content gets delivered, assisting with refunds, and even paying your affiliates. You get paid with direct deposit each week. Your affiliates are the people that get a percentage of every sale in exchange for promoting your material to others. Frequently on Clickbank you'll see products that have 50 percent or greater commissions generated for each sale that an affiliate makes. Since information products have typically 90 percent margin or greater, and there are virtually no delivery expenses, it makes sense to reward your affiliates with a very high commission. Most authors (called vendors or publishers on Clickbank) pay affiliates a high percentage.

## A Book Can Live Much Longer Now. It Doesn't Have to Expire.

Another great benefit of writing e-books is that you can easily update the product at any point and, if you so choose, you can reward your past readers with a brand new copy for free. When's the last time that happened to you as a reader? I've done it numerous times with my e-books.

***Often an E-Book Is Better Than a Real Book***   To be perfectly honest, I'd rather sell an e-book to someone than a real book in most cases. There are several reasons for this, not the least of which is the amount of money that I earn. The book you are now reading had a lot of people touching it before it actually got to you. Everyone gets their piece of the pie including the paper company, the ink company, the glue in the binding company, the printing press business, the marketers, the publishers, the guy that sweeps the publisher's floor at two in the morning, and so on. What does that leave me with in the end? Not much.

With an e-book however, the delivery is instantaneous and free and my profit margins are huge in comparison. That's not the best part of the story though. The best part is when someone buys an e-book from me I get their e-mail address. This means I can follow-up with them and give them current updates, other products and services of interest, and I can begin to build a lifelong relationship with that customer.

Another benefit of an e-book is that I can interact more with the customer. I can include clickable links inside that take readers to blog posts, articles, or other supporting content online. I can even sell something from inside the book, and a click or two later the customer has the product ordered and I have been paid. The book you are now holding can't do that (not even on a Kindle . . . yet).

You can see why I'm such a huge fan of e-books. It probably also makes sense now why I've been writing books for 10 years without ever actually writing a real book.

# CHAPTER 42

# A Targeted Newsletter as a Marketing Machine

**O**ne of the easiest ways to stay in touch with your prospects and customers is to have a regularly published newsletter. For the past several years my own newsletter has been one of my strongest sources of income and influence.

While some businesses may benefit from having a printed and mailed newsletter, I believe that nearly all businesses can and should have an e-mail newsletter. In my case my newsletter is a simple, text-only e-mail that is sent to the customers and prospects that have asked to join my mailing list. Over the years I've had hundreds of thousands of people join that list. Not everyone will stay on the list forever, but those that have stuck around for a long time have developed a great relationship with my business and me.

Here are some of the excuses and issues I run into when I suggest that clients or students of mine begin using newsletters in their business.

## Aren't Newsletters Usually a Waste of Time?

One of the worst things that could happen with your newsletter project is that it would take on a life of its own and become a project that's done simply because it's always been done. It reminds me of the old corporate newsletters that I used to get when I worked for a conventional company. Once every month the newsletter would show up on my desk and I'd watch as everyone nonchalantly dropped their copy of the newsletter into the trash, unless it just so happened that their name or department had been featured that week somehow, and then they'd read that one article. The newsletter simply served the purpose of justifying somebody's job position and provided little other value. That is *not* what your newsletter should become. If it does, then cancel it or change it.

The success of your newsletter can easily be measured by asking two questions:

1. Are your readers happy to get it and then pass it eagerly on to others?
2. Is it generating quality leads and sales for your business with a high ROI for your efforts?

If not, then you are doing something wrong.

The ROI on my newsletter efforts is astronomical. In some cases I've taken 15 or 20 minutes to create an interesting short article teaching a new concept while also selling a related relevant product to my audience. Within a few hours I've made thousands of dollars and the money continues to trickle in over the next several days as the late readers come in.

It's not the newsletter article that was the magic behind those results. It's the trusting relationship with my audience and the size of my audience that are the real factors. The lesson is that you should be building a solid relationship with an ever-growing audience. If the newsletter helps you do that, then it's a worthwhile effort that will pay off in big ways for nearly any business.

## What Should Go in a Good Newsletter?

Your budget, resources, time, and business model are all factors in establishing your newsletter. Perhaps the greatest advice I can give you is to ask your customers what they want before you start your newsletter efforts, and then keep asking them what they want once you have it established. As simple as this advice might seem to be, I'm pretty sure that most businesses that start a newsletter skip this step entirely. The best source of ongoing content will also be your reader base.

One way to know if your newsletter project is going well is to monitor how frequently your newsletter is passed around to other new readers. As part of every newsletter I send out, I invite my readers to forward the newsletter to other people that they think it might help. As a result, each newsletter generates many new e-mail subscribers for me. If this doesn't happen for you, then you need to reevaluate your newsletter efforts.

In order for your newsletter to be worthy of being passed around, you'll need to think from your customers' and prospects' perspective on the topics that you include. Don't waste your time in your newsletter telling your readers how wonderful you are or how great your business is. A newsletter will be evaluated on the quality of the content alone.

### Should I Use a Printed Newsletter or E-Mail?

If you haven't realized by now, I'm a huge fan of e-mail newsletters. I've never actually sent out a print newsletter, although I could. The extra time, expense, and energy involved just don't make it worth it for me. I'm sure I could experiment and make it a profitable model, but e-mail is just so much easier.

Although I am sure there are exceptions to the rule, I am currently unaware of any small businesses that are having raging success with a printed newsletter while ignoring e-mail marketing possibilities.

### I Don't Have Time to Write a Newsletter Every Week!

I don't have time to write a newsletter every week either, so some weeks I just don't. I've never had anyone complain either!

Since I have only an e-mail newsletter for my business I have some advantages.

Some weeks my e-mail newsletter isn't really a newsletter at all. Instead, it's a few brief sentences about an interesting blog post I read with a link directing my readers to go check it out. Other times I just record a quick audio and post it to my blog and then send a short e-mail to my readers letting them know about the new content.

Also, since I use e-mail to distribute my newsletter, I can have multiple newsletters developed in advance and then schedule their delivery easily so that I don't have to write a newsletter for months if I don't want to. That is yet another reason why I'm such a huge fan of e-mail marketing.

### Does Delivery Have to Be Regularly Scheduled in Order for It to Be Effective?

In my opinion, the frequency of your communication with your audience via newsletter is of negligible importance. The real factors of your success are the quality of content, and your ability to engage your audience in beneficial conversations. Send your readers to your blog, or even other websites that don't belong to you, so that they can get all the best information possible on any given subject. It's this type of honest interaction that will build customer loyalty. Once you have that loyalty established your customers won't really care how often you publish. Your newsletter will become an extension of your other content-creating efforts, not unlike your blog, your Facebook page, or your Twitter account.

I go into greater detail about e-mail newsletters in Chapter 54.

# CHAPTER 43

# THINK *FREE* FIRST

Everybody likes free stuff.

No matter how fantastic you believe the quality of your content and information to be, you should strongly consider giving away all of it or nearly all of it entirely for free. If you don't, someone else will anyway, eventually.

I've heard the phrase, "Always be lowering the free line," used to describe this mindset.

Whether you like it or not, customers today expect a whole lot more from you than they ever have before. While you may consider that bad news it's actually a great opportunity for those who understand the power of information and the viral power of free.

## FROM FREE TO FAME

The power of the word "free" eventually led my friend Brian Wampler to partnerships with musical legends like Brad Paisley, Keith Urban, and dozens of other famous musicians and bands that you'd likely recognize.

The story:

For several years my guitar-playing buddy Brian and I worked on houses together, fixing up junkers using loans and investment money from our parents. He had serious construction skills. I mainly did the grunt work.

Neither of us enjoyed this type of work, but we were trying to supplement our income so that we could each work on our true passions online. Luckily for us, we stopped buying houses and started focusing online!

His true passion was guitars and more specifically the tiny niche market of guitar pedal mods (if you've never heard of guitar pedal mods don't worry—it will all make sense in a minute). Working together on houses gave us time to talk, and those talks helped each of us establish what can now easily be considered online empires.

The theme in many of our talks was the power of the word free—and it wound up working out great for both of us!

Ten years ago, bands in the Indianapolis area all knew that there was one local guy who was "the man" when it came to making a guitar pedal produce sounds way cooler than they were supposed to produce. Musicians call these guitar pedal modifications "mods," and Brian was "the man."

Brian would tediously work weekends and evenings on one guitar pedal at a time for band buddies and local musician friends. He made a decent side income charging for his services, but he was trading a few dollars for a few hours, and neither of us would ever settle for that.

As my Internet career began to take off slightly ahead of his, Brian and I had several conversations about how he could use his unique skill to grow a real business around his passion-driven niche.

Enter the free content.

Brian began taking digital pictures and documenting the process he used to modify various guitar pedals and turn them into the valuable "mods" that his local fans were enjoying. He turned these "digital courses" into PDF files that could be easily downloaded or printed and mailed to his increasingly eager fan base. Inevitably, each course that he produced and distributed would lead to more questions, more followers, and more fans of what he was trying to do. The more he distributed this free and inexpensive content online, the more his fan base grew. The demand for his guitar pedal "mods" and manuals, and other related instructional material, began to steadily increase to the point where he had to hire help to meet demand.

Although I'm sure Brian isn't the only guy in the world who can crack open a guitar pedal and modify it with a soldering tool, I am sure he's the only one who took the time to document the process and then give the information away in order to grow a raving fan base.

His reward?

Dozens of the top musicians in the world now use and rave about Brian's Wampler Pedals. He has his own brand on store shelves around the world, and has worked with some of the most talented musicians on the planet, who now rave about his custom equipment.

You can now get the full story at WamplerPedals.com and see where Brian's passion and the word "free" have taken him lately.

By creating a steady stream of current relevant content for your prospects and customers to consume, you are effectively turning them into habitual consumers of your product.

If you're worried about not making any money from all of this free consumption, stop worrying. The real winners in the new economy are those that have large loyal followings. Your business can go in virtually any direction it wants to if it has a large loyal following. The key that will get you access to that reality is free information.

One of my most successful business efforts is a website that was established based on a 100 percent free discussion forum and other quality free content. Word quickly spread online, and before long we had a large audience. A few years later I'm now able to send a short e-mail to all registered members of that site and quickly earn thousands of dollars selling relevant products as an affiliate.

Also consider the business models of Google, YouTube, or Facebook. Let's take Google, for example. Their search engine is free, their e-mail management service Gmail is free, as are hosts of other phenomenal tools. Spend some time thinking about how Google makes its billions and you'll understand the power of free.

## FREE SERVICES

I talked about this concept in Chapter 6 while discussing several irrational habits you should develop. When you give something of value away for free to a prospect or customer, you aren't just giving that one person an opportunity to evaluate you. Thanks to the fact that most of your prospects and customers now have large social networks that they connect with, you are also exposing your overwhelming generosity to potentially hundreds or thousands of other great prospects. It's a lot easier to give a $100 sample to someone if you know for a fact that they're going to go tell several hundred of their friends about the experience. Later in the book I talk about identifying the most socially influential customers so you can treat them like the VIPs that they are. They may not have the look of a VIP, but online there are those that have staggering levels of influence and it pays to get their attention when you can.

When done right, the end result of giving more away is that you'll be forced to raise your prices on your other items because of all the new prospects you'll have. You read another good example of this in Chapter 6 (see Irrational Habit 4).

# CHAPTER 44

# USE A POWERFUL TITLE FOR YOUR MARKETING CONTENT

**O**ne of the great lessons that I learned early on in my business career is the importance of the titles that I chose to use for my information products.

For any information or content that you create, take great care when giving it a name. The name or title of your content is the first impression, and you will gain or lose many readers or viewers based on what you decide to call it.

For example, most professional copywriters will tell you that they spend as much, if not more time, on the title or header of a sales letter than they do on the rest of the entire document. You can assign a lot of value to your content and information if you use powerful words to title it and describe it.

As you begin creating a steady flow of content, keep in mind that the titles you choose are a significant factor in how much impact your efforts have.

Great titles give the content a feel of exclusivity and simplicity at the same time. Creating top 10 lists, or step-by-step lists, make for great content.

**Examples:**
- Seven Things Every Puppy Owner Must Know About Housebreaking
- Five Back Pain Secrets Your Doctor Won't Tell You
- Special Report: Getting Out of Debt, Step-By-Step
- Eight Steps to Landing Your Dream Job Fast

## CHAPTER 45

# YOUR CONTENT DISTRIBUTION STRATEGY

**N**ow that I have you convinced that creating content is a great idea, you're going to need a strategy for distributing your content as widely as possible, in order to give it every chance to be seen or heard by your online prospects.

Distributing your content online isn't a complex task, but it does require someone spending the time to make it happen, or investing in the tools that can be used to help make it happen.

Here are some examples of how your content could be used in smaller ways than it should be, along with some possible solutions:

- It's easy enough to post a video to YouTube.com, but that same video should also be posted to multiple other video-hosting sites in order to gain maximum exposure.
- Creating a quick audio recording of yourself discussing a topic of interest to your readers is simple to do. It's also simple to post that audio to your blog. A good distribution strategy, however, will also include a plan for turning that audio into a transcribed file that can be downloaded and read as well. You could also do a podcast or press release.
- If you go through the trouble of having a regularly scheduled e-mail newsletter, then you should also have a strategy for archiving all of those newsletters somewhere online, where the search engines can see them and they can easily be found online in the future.

These are all examples of how you should be thinking when it comes to distributing your content. There are several great tools that will help you speed up and automate the process of distributing your content as widely as possible. Since these types of tools are always evolving, I include links to some of my favorites on the resource page and then keep those links current as new tools and strategies come on the scene.

Here is an example of a content-distribution strategy.

## JAMIE MCKINNEY, A MARKETING STUDENT OF MINE AT OFFLINEBIZ.COM, RECENTLY REPORTED THESE CONTENT DISTRIBUTION RESULTS TO ME

The client is a lawn sprinkler and landscape lighting installation company.

Jamie built them a simple new website using WordPress, and created several keyword-rich blog posts as part of the site. Next he submitted several articles to article directories using an article distribution tool. Finally he used Animoto.com to create four simple videos by uploading pictures of the work done by the company. These videos contain keyword-rich descriptions.

The results? Jamie's client is now enjoying a new level of exposure and a steady stream of new business. The business is on the front page of Google for the following short- and long-tailed keyword phrases:

- "(Region name) lawn sprinklers" = 5th spot
- "(Region name) lawn irrigation" = 5th spot
- "Lawn sprinklers" = 1st spot in Google Places and 4th spot on front page of Google for anyone performing a search on Google while within the region
- "Lawn sprinkler installation" = 1st and 3rd in Google Places (different addresses) and 7th place on front page
- "(Region name) underground lawn sprinklers" = 1st and 2nd place on front page of Google
- "(Specific region name) outdoor lighting" = 7th and 8th place on front page of Google
- "(Nearby specific region name) outdoor lighting" = 1st and 2nd place on front page of Google
- "(Specific region name) landscape lighting" = 1st and 2nd place on front page of Google
- "Sprinkler systems" = 1st and 2nd place in Google Places for anyone performing a Google search while within the region

# PART 12

# SOCIAL MEDIA MARKETING

The real power of social media kicks in when you find a way to encourage your friends and followers to help you share your message with their own social circles of influence. Earlier in the book I talked about the megaphone that many of your prospects and customers have. Your success in social media is not so much reliant on your ability to use social media to connect with your current customer base, as much as it's reliant on your ability to do or produce something that is worthy of being shared and talked about.

You can also learn a great deal about how social media is being used by everyone from big corporations to small businesses by observing how companies like Starbucks and Dell are using Facebook and Twitter, as well as also paying attention to how it's being used by other small businesses in your niche.

Before hiring anyone to work on your behalf and represent you using social media, be sure to ask them some tough questions, such as who else they have worked with, as well as what success they've had. This is an emerging field, but you want to work with creative people that have a proven track record. What is their strategy to make you and your message shareable?

# CHAPTER 46

# FACEBOOK AS A MARKETING TOOL

**W**hile the marketing potential of Facebook.com is still being discovered and experimented with, we now know for a fact that social media should probably play a big part in most businesses' marketing efforts. Entire books have been written about how to market on Facebook, but in this chapter I attempt to summarize my overall thoughts on Facebook as a marketing tool, and I give you a few tips that I've seen work.

Ultimately your success on Facebook isn't about some magic formula or checklist. It's all about applying the same principles you'd use if you were at a large informal gathering of prospects at a party. You'd never spend your time at a party walking up to each guest and asking them if they will buy something from you, so of course you shouldn't act that way in an online social setting either. Find creative ways to connect with people on social sites and the rest will happen naturally.

As the most popular social media website online, Facebook is visited daily by more people than any other website online as of the writing of this book. This means that you cannot participate in the Facebook community effectively without having an ongoing strategy for interacting with the visitors that your Facebook page will inevitably have. This serves as a caution for you if you're thinking that a Facebook page is something you set up once and then walk away from.

Facebook offers a free "Official Page" to any business, organization, product, musician or band, or celebrity/public figure that wants to set one

up. To see multiple examples of current "Official" pages that are set up, use
this link:

www.facebook.com/pages/browser.php

*You can also set up a "Community Page" around a cause or topic.*
*To set up a new "Official" or "Community" page visit:*

www.facebook.com/pages/create.php

Getting as many fans or followers as possible to click on the "Like"
button on your page is how you rise in the ranks of perceived importance
on Facebook. If enough people "Like" you or your page, a snowball effect
can kick in where your brand or name begin to take on fans that you
otherwise might never have been exposed to.

For example, Einstein Bros., the bagel chain store, offered its customers
free bagels in 2010 if they were simply willing to visit their Facebook fan
page and become a fan. This campaign generated hundreds of thousands of
new Facebook fans for Einstein Bros., but better yet, each of those new fans
exposed the fact that they "Liked" Einstein bagels to their entire respective
social circles on Facebook.

While some marketers might disagree with me (and I know many that
agree), I contend that the best use for your Facebook account is to drive
customers *off* of Facebook and into your lead funnel. This means encouraging them to join your e-mail mailing list, or download your free report,
and so on. The reason I encourage this strategy is simply because Facebook
maintains far too much power over you if you store all of your lead contact
information with them. Facebook reserves the right to shut down any page
on their site at any time, including yours. This has already happened to
many business owners and it could happen to you. Don't be content to
stop with setting up an active Facebook page and think that you are secure.
Also, pay attention to the rules for advertising on your Facebook page. I
won't go into detail here because the rules fluctuate, but Facebook makes
the rules and you'd be wise to understand them, as well as be prepared
for the consequences of even accidentally violating a rule that leads to an
account suspension.

Since Facebook ads are far from free, I won't go too deep into this subject
of using Facebook ads to drive business, although you should know that
there is nothing easy about doing it. I can tell you that setting up a daily
spending budget and being willing to constantly test your ads and landing
pages is vital to success with Facebook advertising, just as it is with any other

paid advertising online. This book is not about those in-depth processes that often carry expensive lessons for the half-informed newbie.

## Some Power Tools for Facebook

www.Hyperalerts.no: Get an e-mail alert when a new post is added to your Facebook page.

www.Fangager.com: Start a rewards program for the fans and followers that interact with you.

# CHAPTER 47

# TWITTER AS A MARKETING TOOL

**T**witter is about instant online conversations viewed and participated in by friends, strangers, and everything in between.

The hesitancy to get on Twitter.com by most businesses and marketers is understandable.

Founder Evan Williams founded Twitter with the basic question: "What are you doing?"

How can the millions of random posts left by millions of users daily possibly be used as a marketing tool? I get into that a bit later in the chapter, but first a few basics, lessons, and warnings about Twitter.

## THE BASICS

On Twitter anyone can say anything they want in short posts added chronologically to their Twitter wall or timeline. If you choose to follow someone on Twitter this means whenever they post a message to their own Twitter wall, that message will also show up on your timeline. Those that follow you will see your posts on their timeline. Everyone gets to pick and choose who they will follow. Typically, celebrities have far more followers than they do people they follow. If you don't have followers it means no one is listening (yet), but all posts are pretty much public material that anyone can search Twitter and see. That's about as simply as I can explain Twitter from my perspective.

Twitter is where millions of users go to build authentic relationships with like-minded people from around the world on any number of various topics. The intricate web of connections that are formed on Twitter are hard to even capture or describe. People gather in groups and follow individuals, causes, events, news, trends, and any other number of interesting topics. If you are interesting, authentic, or are willing to link to others that are, then you can quickly become an effective member of the community that is Twitter.

Twitter is also about participating in real-time conversations. I'm talking about major, breaking news 45 minutes before Fox News or CNN says a word about it. I'm talking about the voices of Iranian voters begging the free world for help in real time, seconds after they've risked their lives protesting corrupt vote counting procedures. If you are the type of person that enjoys openly speaking your mind on such topics you'll enjoy Twitter, even if you aren't into the marketing side of it.

The question for businesses, though, is this: How do you get followers on Twitter that will listen and take a course of action beneficial to you? There are no proven formulas here. We are talking about real people, real relationships, and the randomness of interaction on a one-on-one basis. If you expect only to take from Twitter, you will be disappointed.

Anyone can grab a free account and answer the "What are you doing?" question any way they want to at any time, but Twitter has grown to be a much different tool than simply a way to share with others the details of your breakfast cereal choices. The popularity and stickiness of the site make it a site worth exploring for most of us, and the creative uses of Twitter are still being uncovered.

Personally, I have a love/hate relationship with Twitter.com. I find my e-mail efforts paying far higher dividends currently. While I do have a decent following on Twitter, and I do get on the site several times per week, I'm not convinced yet that my efforts have paid-off to the extent that it's been worth it from an ROI vantage point, but that's not the point. There are users that swear by it, and I am gaining momentum on the site. I'm there for the long term and you can find me @jim_cockrum.

Twitter is a tool best used by those who are willing to be fully authentic in regards to their relationship with their audience. On Twitter there isn't much tolerance for blatant salesmanship in the traditional sense. If you approach Twitter as purely a marketing tool you will likely fail, but if you are interested in pursuing relationships with other like-minded people, or in building your credibility as an expert, then Twitter is a good use of time.

Success on Twitter seems to come easy for those that practice the greatest degree of authenticity and genuine interest in the networking efforts of others, while the whole Twitter experiment feels like time wasted for those with purely selfish or self-promotional goals.

By following and engaging in popular or trending topics that are related to your niche area of expertise, you can gain followers that want to hear more of what you have to say. From there it's up to you to stay real and to build relationships that are mutually beneficial.

**Entire books have been written on the subject of using Twitter, so I won't pretend to capture the full strategy here, but here are some general pointers to keep in mind:**

- Reserve your name now on Twitter (without a space or underscore in the middle) if you haven't yet. Try to get your business name reserved as well, and any short websites (if it will fit), as well as your personal name without spaces. A handle or nickname is often used on Twitter as well, but keep it all congruent with the other online branding efforts you are making. These accounts are free to grab so snatch them up even if you don't plan on using Twitter anytime soon (or ever).
- Use a real picture of yourself in your avatar on Twitter. Make it recent and real. People are very suspicious of faceless avatars on Twitter.
- Ignore the "What are you doing?" premise of Twitter and instead imagine your Twitter followers asking, "Why should I care?" You are correct in assuming that no one really cares what you had for breakfast today unless there is an interesting story or link to a relevant related topic involved.
- Don't treat your followers on Twitter as if they are prospects. Treat them as business acquaintances and colleagues that you are building a long-term relationship with. Once someone joins your mailing list it is okay to develop a prospect/business relationship, but on Twitter keep things more on an informal basis. Many Twitter users resent when Twitter is used as a blatant marketing tool.
- Be shareable. The more observations and comments that you can make that are worthy of a retweet, the better. A retweet happens when someone decides to share your comment with their entire list. This often leads to you getting more followers and influence, so, as often as possible, craft your Twitter posts to be shareable.
- Retweet as often as you tweet. Very few people earn the right to be Twitter snobs and only tweet while the rest of their followers wait eagerly for the next tweet, expecting nothing in return. A retweet is simply helping someone else spread a good tweet. All it takes is a button click.
- Many tools and third party apps have been developed to make the Twitter experience highly customized. I list a few of my favorites

here, but there are literally hundreds of others that can be used. Use Twitdom.com to search through the hundreds of apps that have been set up to help you get the most from Twitter as a communication and lead generation tool.

- Discover creative uses for TweetBeep.com or Search.Twitter.com.

You can easily monitor Twitter for mentions of your brand, name, or keywords related to your services or interests by using the tools found at tweetbeep.com or search.twitter.com.

## Example

Encourage and incentivize customers to post messages about you or your business on Twitter, and then monitor Twitter for the preset key phrases that you've asked them to use. Supposed you have a wall sign that encourages your dining customers to tweet: "Joe's Steakhouse Sizzles," or "My Favorite Steak at Joe's Steakhouse is (fill in the blank)." You should then follow any customer that posts your exact market-friendly message, and reward your most influential Tweeters with incentives and recognition. The process of monitoring popular social sites like Twitter and automating your response to key phrases is becoming a popular marketing strategy for all types of businesses. You can also use a hash-tag (#) in front of a key phrase that identifies you to make finding these comments easier. For example, Joe's Steakhouse above might request that their customers use the hash-tag "#JoesSteak" when making tweets about the restaurant. Chapter 59 has more ideas for rewarding your most socially influential customers.

## Another Example

If your business services a geographic region, set up notifications to be delivered to you or your designated social media manager by e-mail or even by text message whenever someone mentions specific keywords related to your business. At that point engage those customers directly and personally (do it fast while the topic is still in their mind). For example, I just searched Twitter using the site: *search.twitter.com* for this search term: "pizza near: 46143 within: 15mi" and got back about 12 related Twitter posts from the last 45 minutes. These are all people who live within 15 miles of the zip code 46143, and are talking about pizza about an hour before dinner time. Do you think a pizza business would benefit by offering Twitter users some dinner options?

My suggestion for a pizza business would be to automate the process of receiving these types of notifications and then make a very personal and thoughtful effort (not automated) when connecting with these customers as individuals.

- Use TwitScoop.com to monitor Twitter for trends and topics that you feel capable of engaging in conversations about.

With TwitScoop you get a constantly-updated visual representation of what keywords and topics are currently the most popular on Twitter. It's a good way to jump into the hot topics and pick up followers with witty or useful comments on the current news or trends of the day. Frequently you'll see the news happen live on TwitScoop well before it hits the cable news shows or even news websites. For me this is also a great use for that second monitor sitting on my desk.

- Uploading pictures to your Twitter account is an easy and effective way to connect with your audience. Once you have a Twitter account you can upload images via Twitpic.com using your same ID and password that you use for Twitter.com. You don't have to sign up for a separate account with Twitpic. Anyone can leave comments and engage with you about the pictures you upload, so it's a good way to get shareable content onto Twitter.

# CHAPTER 48

# DO SOMETHING VIRAL

**I**f you are fortunate (or unfortunate) enough to do something or see something interesting or shocking enough to garner the interest of the masses, and if you catch it all on video, then congratulations—you could go viral!

There just isn't a proven magic formula that will guarantee you'll be overnight famous, but I'm not convinced that those fifteen minutes of fame would do much for you in the long term anyway.

It's certainly not worth trying to fake your way into fame.

Have you ever watched the show *America's Funniest Home Videos*? Is it just me, or is it pretty easy to tell when someone has tried to make an over-the-top video look candid, but it was really all just a setup? For me, the fun of the show is trying to determine which videos are authentic or accidental, and which ones took 14 different tries to come across as accidents. It's hard to fake that type of reality, so don't waste your time.

Rather than trying to force the issue with viral videos and messages, I suggest you just be your authentic self and create quality content. From time to time you will see an opportunity to be overly generous in how you give of your time or services, and your customers will notice. It's those types of gestures, and commitment to customer service, that will lead to viral exposure for you and your business. Let the crowd do the work for you. They love to tell good stories and spread them around. You just do what you are good at while being as generous as possible.

If you pay attention to the rise of Internet celebrities on YouTube you'll start to notice a trend. Some of them are loud and crazy, some of them are more reserved and introspective, but in all (or nearly all) cases they are honestly presenting themselves. It's that genuine connection that resonates with audiences online. Being passionate about your subject while being genuine is a formula for online viral success that works for anyone.

Rather than trying to make one huge hit, viral video, why not start making short, authentic videos that feature you being genuine about a topic you are passionate about? That approach will make you go viral from multiple little streams of traffic to you, your business, or your cause.

# CHAPTER 49

# OTHER SOCIAL MEDIA TOOLS

**T**here are countless other social media websites online that cater to specific niche audiences or even larger general audiences. Clearly there are only a handful of "big dogs" online right now who appear to be leading the pack. This does not mean that you should ignore the others, nor does it mean that you should spread yourself too thin by trying to be all things to all people.

Let your customers and your prospects guide your decision making in regards to which social media sites you will hang out on and participate in. If there are other social sites that you find to be beneficial for your own self-improvement or advancement, of course use those as well.

However, one of the most basic lessons is that you should be where your audience is. Right now the odds are your social audience is on Facebook and, if any other second choice is an option, then it's probably Twitter. Start on those two for now. Others worth checking out include linkedin.com for professionals, and FourSquare.com if you have a business location that receives walk-in customers.

What are your thoughts on social marketing? How is it working for you? Are there other major sites that should be included? Stop by the book resource page and let us know what you think.

# PART 13

# E-MAIL MARKETING IS AUTOPILOT MARKETING

**O**ne of my catch phrases when coaching businesses or students towards successfully marketing themselves or their businesses is this:

"The only new, semi-techie skill I want to teach you is e-mail management."

Nearly all other technical aspects of your success online can be easily crowd-sourced or outsourced. Sites like odesk.com, vworker.com, and elance.com are all places where you can find a worker to outsource nearly any online project to. You can also use crowd sourcing on sites like mturk.com for any task that can be broken into steps and performed by a crowd for cheap and fast results. When I post a quick question on Twitter or Facebook and allow the crowd to help me out with an issue, I also consider that crowd sourcing. In other words, there's no need to start reading a bunch of books about graphics, programming, and web design in order to be successful on the Internet.

> I'll let you in on a little secret. I've sold and helped sell many millions of dollars of products and services online. I own multiple websites, blogs, membership websites, and lead capture pages but I have no idea how to build a pretty website because I don't have to know that stuff! I don't do techie stuff and neither should you.
>
> But I still think you need to understand the tools of e-mail marketing!

Learning the possibilities and automation strategies behind e-mail marketing is something too important to leave in the hands of anyone else until you grasp it yourself. It's also extremely inexpensive to learn and manage.

Here's why I feel so strongly about it:

I believe that the strongest asset any business can ever have is a large and growing list of loyal followers and partners that *want* to hear from you and *want* to work with you.

Can you think of a better position to be in as a business?

The most efficient long-term strategy for staying in touch with this loyal list is e-mail marketing.

Imagine having over 100,000 e-mail addresses of people that have all asked to be on your e-mail mailing list. You send them useful tips, ideas, and links to content written by you and others on a regular basis and they love you for it. It costs you about $100 per month to manage the whole thing with no other expenses. From time to time you send them offers from you or from others (as an affiliate) and you put $5,000 to $100,000 or more in the bank each time. Sound crazy? I've just described a good portion of my own personal business model. I'm not the only one either. It's the model being used by millions of businesses and professionals around the world right now in one variation or another. I've coached everyone from stay-at-home-moms with a craft business to large real estate offices in major cities on the power of e-mail marketing for one reason: it works.

I know I've said it in other places in this book, but if you *only* read this one section of the book and then put it to use in your business I *promise* you'll owe me a big thank you letter a year from now. Mass e-mail marketing (I didn't just say spam—more on that later) is powerful and you need to integrate it and automate it in your business.

That's a powerful philosophy I've just revealed, and it explains my passion for e-mail marketing.

For the naysayers:

For several years now there have been rumors that e-mail is going away. I think it was the spam issue that got everyone so worked up initially, and then it was the sheer volume that was supposedly going to overwhelm us and turn us off, and then Facebook rumors started swirling, and so on.

My perspective is that e-mail marketing will continue to be where serious conversations and interactions between friends and businesses take place for a long time. Here are some thoughts on the issue:

- Spam is coming under control. It's not that there are fewer spammers, but technology is staying ahead of them, and the law keeps nailing them. E-mail service providers are getting smarter, too. More spam is blocked now than ever, and the ratio of good e-mail getting through is higher than ever for just about every e-mail marketer that I talk to. I love my Gmail.com account. I'd say it's 98 percent accurate on identifying spammers, and when it accidentally calls good e-mail spam, I fix it with a click, and it never happens again with that sender.

- I guess I get way more e-mail than you probably do, but with a bit of organizing effort I stay on top of it quite easily. That's a whole different topic of course, but if a busy guy who operates multiple businesses can stay on top of his e-mail easily, so can everyone else that's paying attention. My point is, e-mail isn't overwhelming to most of us—instead it's a vital communication tool that is here long term.

- Even if we all start to shift away from e-mail someday, you will easily be able to make the transition if you have a large e-mail list because the cost of communicating to your entire list is so inexpensive. Just tell the members of your list where else they can find you. *Note:* Facebook and Twitter *are not* a replacement for e-mail now, nor are they likely ever to be in my opinion.

- You need only to ensure that people *want* to hear from you and you won't have any trouble. Of course, it also makes sense to have other contact info on your prospects and clients. Get as much of it as you can, right down to their second address and fax number if you want to, but e-mail is the least expensive and most effective business marketing tool that has ever been used by humans, so ignore it at your own peril.

- Cutting edge companies, such as Google, continue to pour millions into expanding and managing their own e-mail tools and services that they supply to millions of users worldwide and use themselves. Google is sold on the long-term benefits of e-mail as a serious tool for marketing. By the way: Gmail is by far my favorite e-mail tool and it's free!

Now that I've convinced you that I'm passionate about e-mail and how effective and necessary it is to use it as a marketing tool in *any* business - let's get to work.

## MY E-MAIL MARKETING STRATEGIES AT WORK

"A few years ago I read a piece by Jim on the value and benefits of e-mail marketing. At the time I had a newsletter with a couple thousand e-mail subscribers that was profitable but growing slowly. I started following Jim's tips to aggressively build my list. I created new signup forms, started using auto-responders, started giving away a free e-book to subscribers, and other methods Jim recommends. I also started using eBay to attract viewers to my website and then convert them to subscribers. Today I have over 44,000 confirmed subscribers, and my list and newsletter are responsible for over half the profits of our growing online operations."

Skip McGrath
SkipMcGrath.com
Auction Seller's Resource

# CHAPTER 50

# THE TOOLS AND LANGUAGE OF E-MAIL MARKETING

**E**-mail is the central marketing tool of millions of businesses for a reason. You can inexpensively deliver your message to a virtually unlimited number of prospects with little expense, risk, or downside potential. Ignore the naysayers—e-mail works.

For a few dollars per month you could easily be communicating with hundreds, thousands, or more of your prospects and customers virtually on autopilot. E-mail is the ultimate low-cost marketing tool in my opinion. Is it perfect? No, but it's so close that you are nuts not to use it.

I've used e-mail marketing in my own businesses to the point where I have nearly 50 different e-mail lists that are all automatically accepting new subscribers, and automatically greeting those subscribers with the specific content they've requested. After the initial e-mail is delivered, my customers and prospects automatically receive further e-mail communications, each delivered in a preset order, with preset gaps between the messages. I'm also able to send out a general message to some or all of the prospects on one or several of my lists simultaneously at any point I want to. None of this is complicated if you use a good e-mail management tool.

My favorite e-mail management tool is aweber.com. Spending some time studying the free resources on that website is a good way to familiarize yourself with the language and tools used in e-mail marketing. I also have additional links and information about e-mail marketing on the resource page for this book, including an online video training course that I compiled recently.

Here are a few basic terms (in logical order, not alphabetized) that you'll need to understand in order to effectively speak the language of an e-mail marketer.

*Subscriber*: A subscriber is an individual who has expressed an interest in receiving e-mail from you. Treat your subscribers like people, not like a random e-mail address. Even as your e-mail list grows, you should always write your e-mail messages as if you were writing to one person. A subscriber is a valuable prospect, customer, or partner who has entered into a sacred trust with you, allowing you to interrupt their day with a message whenever you have something of value to share. That privilege can and will be easily revoked at any point when you've stopped earning the right.

*E-mail list*: Any business or customer that I've ever worked with has required at least a handful of lists in order to manage their business properly. Your prospects can go on one list while customers belong on a separate list. Your top customers should all go on their own list as well. Those are just some examples of different lists that you might have within your one e-mail management account. The movement of individuals from one list to another can be automated as well. For example, an online purchase of any kind could trigger a move that lifts an e-mail address from the prospect list and onto the customer list. You can't just put everyone onto one big list and expect to stay relevant. You'll need to segment your lists in as many creative ways as possible in order to be as effective as possible. Don't be intimidated by this process. I have around 50 lists of my own and the segmentation of those lists is done 100 percent on autopilot through my e-mail management service. This is why I suggest you use a good e-mail management service, and also learn the basics of e-mail management.

*Spam*: Spam is a loosely-defined term that is used for any unwanted e-mail that appears in an end user's e-mail box. In my opinion there are two kinds of spam. One of them is a serious matter (easily avoided), and the other, less serious, type of spam needs to be managed but isn't a serious threat to you or your business in any way.

*Serious spam*: Serious spam is generated when someone legally or illegally gathers a bunch of e-mail addresses by purchasing them or pulling them without permission from the Internet either manually or using software that automates the task (called scraping). Even entering e-mail addresses into a computer from a handwritten list, or by any other questionable means can lead to trouble. Even if you are sending relevant messages to such a list, this is potentially considered a serious spam violation and is cause for some concern (or *great* concern if you scraped or bought the addresses). Using a legitimate e-mail delivery service such as aweber.com, getresponse.com, icontact.com, mailchimp.com, or constantcontact.com will virtually ensure that you never violate such serious spam boundaries though. This assurance comes from the fact that these e-mail services do not allow spamming activity to occur on their site, so you can never accidentally engage in it even if you are acting in ignorance and innocence.

*Not-so-serious spam*: Not-so-serious spam happens occasionally to all e-mail marketers. When a fully confirmed subscriber loses interest in your message or forgets who you are and then clicks the spam button in their e-mail control panel by accident, or any other number of strange, similar circumstances lead a subscriber to cry spam, then you have committed a "not-so-serious" spam violation. This happens to small and large e-mail marketers alike and it *will* happen to you. If a significant percentage of your subscribers all accuse you of spam *simultaneously*, then you could have some trouble, but typically only a tiny fraction of any given e-mail broadcast will result in spam complaints if you are handling your e-mail broadcast activities correctly. (With over 100,000 subscribers on my lists I get accused of spamming in a not-so-serious way almost daily.) Typically, with an e-mail blast to my 100,000 prospects, I can easily expect around 30 to 40 spam complaints. No one cares about this low complaint percentage. Subscribers cry "Spam!" all the time, but unless more than .01 percent of them are crying spam at the same time, there is no issue. My e-mail management service tracks it all for me and they don't worry unless more than 1 out of 1,000 people are complaining. I talk in the next chapters about how to conduct yourself correctly with e-mail, but basically it's a simple matter of supplying your subscribers with the information that they request; after that, never get too far off topic in any given message you send out.

*Follow-up sequence*: Each new subscriber that you add to any of your e-mail lists should receive an immediate response back from you (automated, of course) confirming that they've been added to your list. This message should also contain relevant content that lets the subscriber know that they did the right thing in joining your list. After this initial message is delivered, an automatic and preset series of additional messages can then be delivered over time (days, weeks, months or more, if appropriate). These additional messages are called the follow-up sequence. The follow-up sequence of e-mails that any new subscriber receives is vital to your e-mail marketing success, because it allows you to slowly build a trusting relationship with each new subscriber virtually on autopilot.

*Broadcast*: Even as your e-mail list grows on autopilot you will have occasions where you want to send time-sensitive information to the entire list. Maybe you're holding a special sale, or an important event is coming up on the calendar that they all need to know about. This type of one-time e-mail blast is called a broadcast. I broadcast a weekly newsletter to several of the lists that I manage. My e-mail management service automatically ensures that even those subscribers who are subscribed on more than one of my lists each only get one copy of my newsletter when I send a broadcast to multiple lists. For example, if a top customer is on my top customer list as well as my general customer list, they'll only get one copy of my newsletter in their inbox. This list-scrubbing feature is a standard piece of e-mail management tools.

Opt-In: Any legitimate e-mail marketer deals only with opt-in leads. I take it a step further, as do most other marketers I know, and only accept *confirmed* opt-in leads. An opt-in lead is someone who has expressed an interest in joining your mailing list. Many marketers consider this initial expression of interest to be enough of a confirmation to begin sending the new subscriber the content they've requested. The risk you take if you don't confirm each lead, though, is that someone could send you a bunch of junk leads and you would have no way to know if you were spamming the leads or not. To avoid any complications with spam laws I suggest you use confirmed opt-in only. Confirmed opt-in is the process where you automatically respond to an initial subscription request with a confirmation e-mail. Unless the prospect takes the action requested in the confirmation e-mail, they will receive no further communication from you. This will mean fewer subscribers ultimately, but you will avoid entirely any e-mail address misspells, or a mean competitor trying to get you into spam trouble by adding a bunch of bad addresses to your list. My list of over 100,000 subscribers has been built using confirmed opt-in so I have virtually *no* spam worries. The only way I could be accused of spamming is if I go *way* off of message in my communications to my list and start talking about pig farming to an e-mail list built around parenting tips.

Opt-Out: One of the regulations that all e-mail marketers must follow is to provide a way for your subscribers to easily opt-out of receiving any further messages from you. This clickable link must be visibly present inside of each message that goes out. It's rules and laws like this that lead me to suggest to you that you allow a third-party service, such as the ones I've mentioned, to manage your e-mail lists and mailings for you. Any reputable e-mail management service will automatically insert an unsubscribe link at the bottom of every message that you send out.

*Web Form*: A web form is also sometimes called an opt-in form. It's simply the data form that a potential subscriber will use to join your mailing list. You could ask for just an e-mail address on your web form, or require much more information (name, etc.). The less you ask for, the better your opt-in rate will be though. For example, I have a squeeze page at SilentJim.com that contains a basic web form for gathering e-mail addresses for my newsletter. I ask simply for a name and e-mail address. Most people just give me a first name instead of a full name, but that's all I need.

# CHAPTER 51

# AUTOMATED POWER MARKETING: CUSTOMER AND PROSPECT E-MAIL

Once you understand the basics of e-mail marketing you can begin to easily follow-up with customers and prospects automatically. Like I said, I manage over 50 e-mail lists in my business on complete autopilot. On any given day we have hundreds of different subscribers joining different lists and even moving automatically from one list (prospect list) to another list (customer list) seamlessly.

However, I won't get into the semitechnical details of setting all of this up, because that information can easily be found on the websites of any of the services mentioned in this part of the book. But I can tell you some of the lessons I learned about following-up with my customers and prospects using e-mail.

No matter how small your business is, you should use e-mail in as automated a way as possible. For example, the vacation settings in a free Gmail account can be used to instantly reply to every customer that sends you an e-mail. The reply e-mail could have a link to a special offer or to a blog site with additional information. That is about as simple as e-mail automation gets, but it's better than nothing. Of course you'll still reply to each customer with a personal message after they get the autoreply.

For the rest of this chapter, though, I'm going to assume that you are interested in using a serious e-mail management tool, such as aweber.com, or any of the other e-mail services that I've listed on my resource page.

# KEEP IT SHORT

A great rule of thumb with e-mail is to always keep it short. Even if you have a great article, newsletter, or other important information to share, you should always keep your e-mail communications short and sweet. For example, when I write a great blog post it's rare that I send the entire blog post out in an e-mail broadcast. Instead I write a short description of the article in a couple of sentences and then include a link for more information in my e-mail broadcast. This type of broadcast message is far less likely to generate spam complaints, and it also increases the traffic to my blog, where I can present the information in a more attractive fashion. On the blog I can interact with the readers in the comment section of my blog post.

# HTML IS PRETTY, BUT DON'T DO IT

There is an ongoing debate about using plain text e-mail versus HTML graphics to create pretty e-mail. I fall firmly in favor of the camp of simple, plain text messages, as do most other marketers that I work with. E-mail management services like to try to sell other services (and some of them even throw it in for free), but I still don't use HTML-pretty messages. I won't go into all of the reasons here, but a couple of the strongest arguments I have are the fact that HTML e-mail messages are clearly more likely to get caught in spam filters, and they also instantly identify you as being a business and not a person. I try to keep my e-mail communications personal and friendly. I want my subscriber to completely forget the fact that 100,000 other readers are also reading the same message they are. A plain text message looks like the e-mail they just got from Grandma, and I want it that way. If I want to send something fancier to my customers, I simply include a link to the fancy website, but I don't send them a fancy e-mail. I know this approach isn't right for every business but it's a perspective to keep in mind, and it works very well for me.

# WHAT DO I SEND THEM?

When you first begin using e-mail automation you'll need to establish a series of short, powerful, informational messages that can be sent out in a series over time. In the previous chapter I told you about using a follow-up sequence. There should be a gap of a few days in between each message, and your messages should be 70 to 80 percent informational, and only 20 to 30 percent sales-oriented, at most. I suggest that the first several messages do absolutely no selling whatsoever; instead you giveaway a bunch of great relevant content that builds the customer's trust in your creativity and leadership in the niche market you are writing about.

Referring customers to a popular blog article that you've written (or that someone else has written) and asking them what their thoughts are on the article is a great example of an informational message that leads to interaction and then builds trust. Every new customer gets the same series of e-mails, and they all get sent to the same article, and they all get to see the comments and interaction occurring simultaneously. This builds a sense of community and trust among your subscribers. It shows them who you are, what you are all about, and that they aren't alone. Ask plenty of open-ended questions in these messages as well, and engage with those that respond. Your e-mail communication shouldn't feel like a company brochure, but instead like a conversation with friends. I want you to blend in with the rest of the messages that your prospects *want* to see in their inbox. For this reason I also suggest that you use your name and not a biz name in the From field.

## Duplicate Yourself with E-Mail

As I've attended various conventions and Internet-related events around the world, it has been interesting to see how powerful and effective my e-mail efforts have been in solidifying my name and reputation in the minds of my readers. It's not uncommon to have people walk up to me and reference an e-mail from me that they got a few days ago, and they'll begin discussing it with me. The fact is, though, I wrote that e-mail and article over two years ago, inserted it into my follow-up sequence, and yet the reader thinks I just recently wrote and sent them that article. This is a powerful phenomenon that nearly any business can and should put to use.

## This Sounds Like a Lot of Work, Doesn't It?

The beauty of automating your e-mail follow-up sequence is that you can do it one time and then leave it all on autopilot indefinitely. Each new prospect that signs up will begin getting a long series of relationship building messages from you, and you will reap the rewards if done correctly. If this sounds like too much work, let me remind you of a couple things. If you are going to build a relationship with a prospect it is going to take multiple contacts with them. This is likely something you've heard before now, right?

Marketing studies have been telling us for years that it takes multiple points of personal contact with prospects before they begin to trust a business or organization. Wouldn't it be better if you could alleviate some of the responsibility of these multiple contacts by automating the process somewhat or entirely? Do the work one time and then reap the reward indefinitely. This is the best kind of business strategy.

***How to Get It Done***    Dedicate a couple of days to sitting down and thinking through the 20 most useful and most relevant topics that your prospects are likely interested in, and then put together short e-mail messages that point your prospects to further information on those subjects. The full article could be on your blog, or you could make your point quickly in a short e-mail article. If you aren't sure what to write about, then conduct a survey of your current top customers to find out what most interests them. Over time you can always add to the series of messages as well. Once you have this task complete you'll have a virtual top salesman in place who will be winning people over little by little with quality information and advice while asking nothing in return. When it comes time to make a sale your customer will be more than ready to listen to what you have to say, if they don't track you down first because of all the great info you've been sending them!

# CHAPTER 52

# MANAGING YOUR E-MAIL
# ON AUTOPILOT

**I**'ve dedicated a significant portion of this book to convince you that e-mail marketing is a vital part of any business or organization's marketing efforts because of how inexpensive and highly effective it is. However, the biggest mistake you can make in pursuing e-mail marketing as a strategy is to make it a manual process. The basic skills and tools for automating your e-mail efforts are vital if you are to get the full benefit from your efforts.

**Here are the basics tools you'll need to understand in order to automate your e-mail marketing system:**

1. An e-mail management service.

There are two types of e-mail management systems you can deploy in your business. There are hosted solutions, and then there are solutions that allow you to store all of your data on your own computers and send e-mail from your own servers. I'm a big fan of paying a reputable e-mail service to host all of my addresses and manage my accounts for me. There are several benefits in going this route including:

- Your solution provider ensures that you remain compliant with all current spam laws.
- You don't have to worry about your IP address becoming blacklisted, or other issues surrounding the management of mass e-mail marketing efforts.
- You automatically stay on the cutting edge of new tools and options without having to upgrade your hardware or software to accommodate the changes.

While some marketers enjoy being able to manage their e-mail addresses themselves from their own computers, I prefer to out-source this entirely because it alleviates so many potential problems from my business. Also, I can export my entire database from my e-mail service provider anytime I want to—it's not as if they own my e-mail addresses. To me it feels like keeping my money in a bank rather than keeping it under my own mattress.

2. Squeeze pages and opt-in forms.

In Chapter 7 I discuss squeeze pages and opt-in forms thoroughly. Briefly, a squeeze page is a simple, one-page website designed with one purpose in mind. The purpose is to gather e-mail leads. The most important part of a squeeze page is the opt-in form, where prospects enter their contact information and then immediately begin receiving the follow-up messages you have preset in your e-mail management account. If you are going to automate your e-mail marketing efforts, you will need to send prospects quality squeeze pages that contain an e-mail opt-in form.

3. Set up automation inside your accounts.

As prospects become customers, and then customers become VIP customers, they begin receiving different types of e-mail messages from you. Ideally, you have established automation rules inside of your e-mail management account so prospects automatically shift from one list to another. For example, you can tie your website check-out system to your e-mail management service and automatically move any prospect onto the Recent Customer list when they make a purchase from you.

4. Your follow-up messages.

As new prospects are added to your e-mail lists you begin sending them a series of preset messages that arrive sequentially. Sometimes this is referred to as a *drip campaign*. Any e-mail management system such as the ones I've already told you about can accommodate such a set-up.

## A Winning E-Mail Strategy

Remember, the most important factor in the success of your e-mail marketing campaign will be your ability to establish trust and rapport with your audience over time. If you fire out a series of sales pitch messages, your e-mail marketing efforts will be a failure. Since the entire process is auto-mated you can afford to win your customers over slowly, by giving them fantastic content and quality tips spread out over multiple messages, before you even attempt to sell them anything.

# CHAPTER 53

# GROWING YOUR E-MAIL LISTS ON AUTOPILOT

In my own online businesses I focus heavily and strategically on constantly growing my e-mail lists with a steady stream of new prospects. Every day I add a minimum of 100 to 200 new prospects into my various e-mail lead funnels. This level of continuous growth does not happen by accident. I've set-up several systems that drive this type of traffic to my e-mail opt-in pages.

While every organization and niche market will be a little different, there are several effective strategies that can be used to grow an e-mail list by anyone. Here's an example of one of my students having success growing his e-mail list in a tiny, strange "niche," but it's an example of how broadly useful e-mail marketing strategies can be.

> My site is TacticalPaintballSniper.com and the niche is Extreme Sports. My target customers are guys (98 percent male) that love their gear, their camouflage, and their tactical gameplay.
>
> In 2010 I launched the site that started out as just a blog. I have a quirky and particular set of skills and training in this area, and I wanted to reach out and deliver some of this experience to other enthusiasts. I strategically set out to build my mailing list first and then survey them to find out what else they were interested in. My goal was to deliver relevant content to them while building a great relationship with my fans. Eight months after launching I had a list of 900 e-mail subscribers and 556 loyal Facebook fans. For the statistics junkies out there, when I send out an e-mail I get about a 31 percent open rate and roughly 15 percent click on my links. This can get as high as 50 percent with certain topics.

My favorite part about the whole experience has been the conversations I get to have with people who share my interests! I've had some awesome e-mails from all over the world, from fans responding to my videos, articles and sharing stories.

There are three key strategies that I have used from the beginning. I put these ideas into practice from what I learned in the e-mail list building course by Jim Cockrum (ListBuildingClass.com). I have only begun to scratch the surface for leveraging these strategies, and they form the cornerstone of what I'm doing.

1. Find other key players in your niche with already established lists and begin to talk to them about sharing information. As an example, I found a major gear supplier and joined his Facebook page. I interacted there, posted some helpful information, complemented his work, and just generally did the things that we should all be doing in any important relationship. I sent him a private message one evening and asked to do an interview with him on gear selection and tuning for my members. He was totally into it and we posted and shared a 45-minute interview with my list of (then) 500 subscribers and his list of 8,000! That was awesome exposure for me.

2. Talk to the individual rather than the list. As you begin to interact with people online, remember, they are people—they are not a list! When you write or create videos, do it as though you're talking to one person. And when you get private messages from your members (and you will), respond personally and quickly. Write with a smile and let them know you value them. They will spread the word and you'll be amazed at the opportunities that will begin to open up!

3. Be consistent and be brief. Never let more than a week or two go by without interacting with your people in some way. The online world is fast-paced and you will quickly be forgotten if you are quiet for too long. When you do interact, respect the time and needs of your audience. Deliver very actionable and practical information, tips that they can put to work right away. Time is easily wasted online and your subscribers deserve respect for their time by delivering only quality content.

Building a list has been, for me, an incredibly satisfying experience. In just a few short months I went from zero Internet presence to an expert in my niche with a large following. It has opened up a ton of opportunities—more than I can actually handle! The process has provided a template for me to do it again and again in my other favorite niches.

Doug Kramer
TacticalPaintBallSniper.com

Here are several strategies I personally use, along with a brief description of each. You'll find further information about many of these strategies throughout this book.

- Partner in creative ways with those that already have an e-mail list.

    One of the most powerful strategies for quickly growing your own e-mail list is to find creative ways to partner with those that already have a large e-mail list that contains good potential prospects. These types of cooperative partnerships are often called joint ventures or JVs. If you are starting without any e-mail list of your own, you will have to be creative in how you approach potential partners. You will have to find a way to make the list owner look good or earn a nice income for them in order for them to be interested in allowing you access to their list. For example, you might create a high-quality special report and allow the list owner to put their name on the cover as your co-author. Interviewing them and requesting that they share it with their own list is also a great idea. Next, the list owner passes the report or interview out to their entire e-mail list. This makes them look good, and you will grow your e-mail list because of the call to action that is found inside of the special report. The best call to action is something like an offer for more content or free updates of the special report. More info is in Chapters 66 and 67.

- Write quality articles.

    Creating quality content and distributing it online far and wide is useful for more than just generating traffic or recognition for your name and websites. I feel strongly that the best signature line any article can have should include a link to a squeeze page or opt-in page, so the readers of the article can instantly join your e-mail list if they are interested in the content they just read. I would rather have one new e-mail subscriber as a result of someone reading my article as opposed to 100 random website visitors that only stop by my site and are then gone forever. More info on this is in Chapter 73 and in Chapter 39.

- Submit quality videos to popular video hosting services.

The statistics are astounding. People are increasingly consuming on-line video content at a rapid pace. Rather than have your videos viewed once and then lose the prospect/viewer forever, why not include an invitation to join your e-mail list as a strategic part of every video you produce? More info on this is in Chapter 88, as well as in all of Part 10.

- Keep an active blog.

    In my opinion the fastest way to measure the effectiveness of a blog is to ask one simple question. How many loyal readers does it have? If a blog has a significant number of readers, yet there is no e-mail capture activity occurring, the blog owner is throwing away literally thousands or possibly even millions of dollars of potential business or publicity. The best call to action for any blog is to encourage blog readers to join the e-mail mailing list. Perhaps the only thing you will ever use those e-mail addresses for is to notify your fans each time there is a new article, but the time will come when you will certainly find it very helpful to have instant access to your entire audience for some other purpose. More info about this is in Chapter 10.

- Swap blog articles with those that have popular blogs.

    It's quite common for bloggers to request a blog article swap with other bloggers in the same niche area of interest. You should pursue this type of blog swap activity, but with a twist. Whenever you provide an article to another blogger, be sure to include an invitation to join your e-mail newsletter list as part of the article. You'll likely need to ask the permission of the other blogger before doing this, but typically they will agree because most people don't mind and don't care about (or even understand) e-mail marketing and how powerful it is. More info about this is in Chapter 72.

- Create simple information products for wide distribution online. I'm often asked why I am such a big fan of distributing free content online. The reason is quite simple. If you can pass out quality, free information on the Internet, then you can easily convince your prospects to give you an e-mail address. From there it's just a matter of time before you win them over and convince them that you are the go-to expert on your niche topic of interest. The more free, quality content that you can distribute on the Internet, the more likely you are to pull in the types of prospects that your business needs. More info on this topic can be found in Part 11.

- Attracting new prospects on eBay.

    Most people see eBay as a big yard sale where random items are bought and sold by millions daily. I see eBay in an entirely different light. I see eBay as a source of new e-mail prospects and leads for virtually any business. Rather than teach my new students how to build their own websites or sell their own products online, I frequently encourage them to begin in a much simpler forum where the traffic is virtually guaranteed. That forum is eBay. You can pull in multiple leads with just a handful of auctions strategically positioned on eBay. More info about eBay is located in Chapter 25.

- Search Engine Optimization (SEO) efforts. While I'm not a big fan of spending a whole lot of energy or money on search engine optimization efforts, I can tell you what the best use of any exposure you happen to get is: If you have websites that rank well on the search engines, thanks to either your tenacity or good fortune, the best use of that exposure (however temporary it may be) is to generate as many e-mail prospects as you possibly can from all of the traffic they generate. More info on this topic is in Chapter 14.

- The best use of free press. On those occasions where you or your business are featured in some type of press interview, article, or television appearance, you need to be prepared. If you are allowed to mention a reference to one of your websites or services, the best thing you can possibly mention is a simple squeeze page designed to gather the e-mail addresses of prospects in exchange for additional information on the topic that you were covering. In my own business, the website SilentJim.com typically serves this purpose. Giving away a high-quality information product before you even ask for an e-mail address is also a strategy that is gaining popularity, as people become more protective of their contact information. More info can be found in Part 7.

- Ask your e-mail subscribers to forward your messages. As your e-mail list begins to grow there is a synergy effect that will begin to take place. If you are sending out good information, there is a good chance that your subscribers will forward the information on to other friends and colleagues that might also benefit or enjoy your mailings. You can multiply the effect by intentionally encouraging them to distribute your information with each e-mail you send. Make it as easy as possible for new subscribers to join your mailing list as part of each message that you send out. For example, in each of my newsletters I say, "If someone forwarded you this e-mail please take a moment to visit SilentJim.com so that you can get on our free mailing list as well."

- Invite every buying customer to join your list.

Perhaps the best time to invite someone to join your mailing list is at the point of purchase. Some examples: a sign hung near the register of a retail store, a printed invitation at the bottom of each receipt, or even trained staff, who verbally explain your e-mail customer appreciation program to each new customer. Any of these tiny procedural shifts can reap huge benefits in growing your e-mail list and eventually having a huge impact on your business.

- Get creative with your account names. Whenever possible I use the name *SilentJimDotCom* as my account name or handle for services or forums that I join. You never know when a new subscriber will lead to thousands of dollars of new business, so it can really pay to get every extra bit of attention to your squeeze page and e-mail list that you possibly can.

# CHAPTER 54

# AN E-MAIL NEWSLETTER CAN BE A CASH GENERATOR

I still vividly remember the day I became convinced that I should start my own e-mail newsletter. I had no subscribers, and no idea where I would find subscribers, but I was very convinced that this was something I was going to do. It was probably the best career decision I've ever made.

Industry statistics tell us that when e-mail marketing is done correctly you can expect a 50:1 ROI ratio. This means for every dollar spent you'll be earning $50. That's just too good to ignore.

Once you have e-mail addresses, what is the best way to maintain contact with the people that have entrusted you with their contact information? One great answer is a simple e-mail newsletter.

After maintaining my own e-mail newsletter for nearly a decade now, I have learned several things about what does and doesn't work. If you are considering starting an e-mail newsletter keep these ideas in mind:

- When writing a newsletter be sure to put in indicators that help your readers to know that the content is current. This is the opposite advice that I gave you concerning your follow-up messages. Your follow-up messages will be the same for every subscriber no matter how far into the future they might join your list. In contrast, your newsletter is a one-time, relevant snapshot of current issues and events, so specific dates, times, and time sensitive info is acceptable.
- You don't have to be a writer in order to have a very effective e-mail newsletter. Your e-mail newsletter could easily consist of a short message and a link directing your readers to your latest video posted

on YouTube. You could also simply record yourself talking about your subject matter and then upload that audio (MP3 or WAV file) to the web, and link to it in your newsletter. I use the term *newsletter* loosely; I'm not even sure I like the word to describe your broadcasted e-mail communications. Just because I call my weekly mailings a newsletter does not mean I deliver a traditional newsletter-looking e-mail to my prospects every week.

- Your newsletter does not have to look fancy in your readers' inbox. I actually discourage my students and clients from using fancy templates when sending e-mail. It's okay to link to a fancy-looking newsletter from inside your e-mail newsletter, but the disadvantages of using HTML templates are well-documented, in my opinion.

- The best source of ideas for content in your newsletter is your reader base. Survey them frequently to ensure that you are staying relevant and to get new ideas for content.

- Long e-mail newsletters just don't work. If you have three or four great articles to share with your audience in your e-mail newsletter, please don't send them all in one long e-mail! You should instead include short excerpts from each article along with a link where your readers can go to read the full article (ideally on your blog). This will increase your overall readership and will also make your messages far more likely to make it through the spam filters. Spam filters are used on all major e-mail services and they all tend to block long e-mails more frequently than they block shorter e-mails.

- Try not to go more than two weeks or so in between contacts with your e-mail list. Setting up automated follow-up messages will help ensure that your readers are hearing from you frequently and that they are receiving good content.

- There is no such thing as 100 percent delivery, 100 percent open-rates, 100 percent happy subscribers, or 100 percent "spam accusation freedom." It's all part of the game. Remember—as long as you are *only* dealing with subscribers who have expressed a specific interest in receiving e-mail from you, you are safe to use e-mail as a promotional tool, but there is nothing perfect about e-mail as we all know. Important messages will sometimes get lost or blocked, people will forget who you are or why they subscribed, lazy subscribers will click the spam button instead of unsubscribing, and you will get occasional complaints from people who think you should be doing things differently. This is all just part of maintaining a one-to-many marketing project such as an e-mail newsletter. I had to learn to have thicker skin—it's a life skill that all entrepreneurs must develop.

- While your prospects certainly expect you to try to sell them things in your newsletters, keep your ratio of content-to-sales pitch at about 80/20. This means 80 percent of what goes into every newsletter is purely informational content. Once you've established the tone of your e-mail messaging, stick with it. I had to learn this lesson the hard way. My e-mail communications with my readers is typically about 90 percent business-related and only 10 percent personal and other topics. In one particular newsletter a few years ago I spent an unusual amount of time discussing an important family/personal issue. While I received an overwhelming amount of supportive responses from my readers, I also received a record high level of spam complaints. I could probably interpret this as either being positive or negative, but instead I'm just presenting it to you as the reality of having an established expectation level. Once you go outside of the norm, you can expect a response that may not be what you were planning on.
- Learn to stay on topic. I see many e-mail marketers falsely assume that their subscribers are interested in all topics even loosely related to the original content that they signed up for. Proceed with great caution into these types of subjects. Before you blast a questionable article or offer out to your entire list, you should probably test it on a handful of subscribers first and see what their response and reaction is. Just because you've earned the right to be influential in one area of your subscribers' lives does not mean you've earned the right to influence them in all other related (or, heaven forbid, entirely unrelated) areas. Respect the boundaries or your readers will drop out or, worse yet, click the spam button. It's just human nature.

If you have a new topic you'd like to introduce to your readers, allow them to voluntarily add themselves to the new mailing list. This sort of segmentation makes it far easier to communicate with your list. You can *never* be over-segmented. It's an established rule of e-mail marketing.

- You don't have to stick to a predetermined schedule for your newsletter. While I tried to get my newsletter out every week, I've never had anyone complain when I skipped a week or two on occasion. People are busy and they aren't going to mind, and very few will even notice, if they don't get their newsletter.
- If the newsletter isn't making you money, or building customer loyalty that leads to increased sales in some way, then it is a waste of time and your efforts should be reevaluated. E-mail marketing, done

correctly, should be very lucrative as well as being a great experience for customers.

- As you add new editions of your newsletter be sure to post them online somewhere where they can be seen and indexed by the search engines. The e-mail management service I use does this for me automatically, as do most other e-mail delivery tools.

# CHAPTER 55

# ADD HUNDREDS OR THOUSANDS OF E-MAIL SUBSCRIBERS QUICKLY

A slow and steady stream of new subscribers constantly being added to your e-mail lists is far preferred over making any stupid decisions that could lead to violations of the law, your websites being banned, and your name or reputation being tarnished. Never buy e-mail addresses or send e-mail to a list that someone gives you.

The quickest way to legitimately add hundreds or thousands of new e-mail subscribers to your opt-in list is to find a good partner that already has a large e-mail following and then work with them in a creative way.

In Part 16 of this book I discuss in greater detail some of the strategies you can use to find great partners, so I won't go into much detail on that subject here.

By fashioning an offer that makes the list owner look good, while also inviting subscribers to join your e-mail list, you can generate many new subscribers virtually instantly. I've helped many up and coming experts get their own mailing list started by using variations of this idea. I've also grown my list significantly on several occasions by approaching other list owners with appealing ideas.

I realize that the title of this chapter may have led you to believe that there was some secret strategy you could use to instantly grow a huge loyal mailing list. After 10 years in this industry I can tell you in no uncertain terms that there is no such strategy that I'm holding back from you. It's all right here. I do offer a course on the book resource page if you want to see more of the details of how I develop and manage my ever-growing e-mail list, but success is based on applying the strategies I'm revealing in this book.

The only other successful strategy that I've ever heard of for adding multiple subscribers quickly is by using traditional advertising strategies, such as a postcard campaign to drive traffic to a good e-mail opt-in page. That approach requires testing and some investment to accomplish, and I've never done it myself. If you've had success with that strategy, please share your story with us on the resource page for this book.

## PART 14

# WHO'S DRIVING YOUR BUSINESS?

$S$ome of the best advice I received early on in my Internet business career was to frequently survey my followers to help set the course going forward. It's just not necessary to continually have to make guesses about what your customers and followers want and expect from you. I'm not saying you should move away from your core purpose or business, but it sure helps to know what your customers and followers are thinking.

**Respected marketing expert Marlon Sanders taught me early on in my online career about his simple success formula for information marketers that goes something like this:**

Step 1. Grow your audience
Step 2. Ask them what they want
Step 3. Give them what they want
Step 4. Repeat

I am consistently surprised by the responses I get when I survey my audience about what they think I should be working on next. The greatest source of inspiration, creativity, content, and direction for my business has come from my newsletter and blog followers.

# CHAPTER 56

# USING A SURVEY AS A MARKETING TOOL

Very simple online tools can be used to quickly determine what's on the minds of your prospects and followers.

Even a simple free tool like surveymonkey.com can be used to get into the minds of your customers and prospects.

Often times when I am at the point where I am unsure which project or product I should be focusing my attention on, I turn to a survey to get the answer. Not only do surveys tell me what my customers are most interested in, but I can also determine what price points I should be using by simply asking my readers their opinions.

I've often found that a good survey can also be a good marketing tool all by itself, even before I analyze the results. For example, one of the questions I might ask my reader base would be: "One of the most common requests I get is for a course on how to set-up your own automated e-mail marketing campaign. While I already sell a popular course at ListBuildingClass.com on this topic, would you be interested in a series of live call-in Q/A training sessions on that topic? If so, what would you be willing to pay in order to keep it exclusive, with a limited number of live participants?"

Sorry for the blatant promotion in that sample question, but that's the whole point. While I'm collecting usable data I'm also telling those taking the survey about the products and services I already offer.

There are several free and low-cost online survey tools that can easily be found with a quick search on Google. The free features of surveymonkey .com have done the job for me on several occasions, though. I highly recommend their services for conducting surveys.

# CHAPTER 57

# GIVE THEM WHAT THEY WANT

For those that make a regular habit of listening to their customers and then making business decisions based on that feedback, this chapter may seem unnecessary.

I would venture to guess, however, that most people reading this book right now have never actually surveyed their customers or followers in order to find out what they are thinking. Instead you rely on your instincts.

While I'm not telling you to move away from your current core values or principles just because of some survey results, I am telling you that you can learn a lot from a simple survey. You can then decide after the survey if you want to ignore or act on the results.

As a result of surveying my readers I've discovered several interesting facts that I was previously unaware of. For example, when I asked my reader-base how often they wanted to receive e-mail tips and ideas from me, I was surprised to learn that the vast majority of them wanted to hear from me "whenever I had something valuable to share," as opposed to the other options, such as, "once per week," or once every "two weeks." I also discovered that customers are willing to pay far more money for my services and training if there is an exclusive feel to the training. As a result, I've successfully offered courses for $1,000 per person and limited the class size to just 30 people. I was confident that the class would sell out because my customers had told me that they were interested in that price point as long as the class was kept relatively small. There is no need to guess about these types of decisions.

At any given time, most entrepreneurs have multiple possible projects on their mind. Why not let your customers help you pick which project you tackle next? By including your customers in the decision-making process you are warming them up to the idea of the new service or product that you will bring to them.

# CHAPTER 58

# REMEMBER WHO IS IN CHARGE

*The richest man is not he who has the most, but he who needs the least.*
—Unknown Author

**I**f you are too busy running your business to find time to market your business, then something is wrong. You should be working *on* your business and not *in* your business.

The best ideas for solving problems, growing your business, and even marketing your business are likely to come while you are *not* working.

It may seem strange, but one of the best ways to grow your business might be to stop working so hard.

## ABOUT PLAYING AND EXERCISING

Maybe this story that I saw online in a few different places recently will help illustrate my point. One of the richest business owners in the world, Richard Branson, was supposedly asked a simple question: "What can someone do to become more productive?" According to the story, his answer was simply, "Work out." He claims that he adds an extra four hours of productivity every day because he takes time to exercise.

I can attest to the fact that this is true in my life, as well. At least two or three times per week you'll find me forcing time into my schedule for serious exercise. When I get out of the habit of exercising, my mood, productivity, and energy level drop. Ask anyone that exercises regularly and they'll tell you the same thing. They have more energy, creativity, and productivity when they work out, and when they stop it all starts to slow down. You will never be at your best unless you make time to work up a sweat on a regular basis. If a book on marketing is the final push that encourages you to get going, then I consider this book a big success.

One of my marketing mentors, Marlon Sanders, encouraged everyone in his audience to "play" on a regular basis. I've never heard anyone encourage a group of adults to be sure and include playtime in their schedule. As it turns out, both exercise and entertaining play release endorphins into your system. The benefit of a regular boost from endorphins is well documented as a creativity and productivity booster. I think you'll find, as I have, that the best ideas, solutions, and creative bursts of genius will come to you when you are playing or working out, not when you are sitting behind your computer monitor.

If you want to be a leader and be perceived as an expert, you are going to need to show some discipline in your schedule. One of the best signs that someone is the master of their schedule is the fact that they take time to work out and take care of themselves.

# PART 15

# Spoiled Prospects and Customers Are Loyal

Thanks to technology it has never been easier to keep track of and maintain relationships with a large number of customers and prospects and wow them on a regular basis. This is true no matter how small your businesses is or how limited your budget or staff.

If you aren't in the habit of maintaining regular contact with your top customers and, even more importantly, spoiling them with special offers, discounts, and even personalized birthday cards, then you are missing out on a great opportunity. Companies that provide this sort of customer service have always stood out from the crowd, but now the stakes are even higher and the benefits are even bigger because of the large social networks that your customers are all part of. If you are in the habit of spoiling your customers, word can spread very quickly. Here are some examples.

## Jing

Take ten minutes to get comfortable with the free and very simple to use screen capture/recording tool called Jing (techsmith.com/jing). This simple tool allows you to produce short videos with your webcam, or by screen capture (it films whatever is on your screen when you turn it on).

Once it's installed, you can capture short videos in response to customer e-mail inquiries. For example, if a customer inquires about one of your products, take a quick video of yourself holding up the product and answering their question. With Jing it will take you less than one minute to shoot the video, upload it, and include a link to the personalized video hosted on the Jing server.

I've blown away customers and prospects using this strategy and it only takes a few seconds longer than if I'd used a typical e-mail response.

# FOURSQUARE.COM

FourSquare.com is a mobile phone app that allows the user to earn points and recognition for visiting different locations and checking in there. For example, the most frequent visitors to any given location get recognized online as the Mayor, and so on.

In 2010 FourSquare took off. That year they registered over 380,000,000 check-ins globally, in every country on earth except North Korea. They are poised to expand rapidly because of the social and engaging nature of the service. Any business that takes walk-in clients would be wise to participate, as well as to encourage their clientele to get in on the fun of FourSquare.

FourSquare's free set of tools for business owners can help attract new customers and keep the regulars coming back loyally. Businesses from national chains to mom-and-pop shops are embracing the marketing power of FourSquare. You can offer specials and mobile coupons (discounts that are automatically presented when users check-in), or even prizes for the 10th visit, and so on. Some businesses reserve parking spots for the Mayor, who is the customer that checks in the most on FourSquare.

These are examples of embracing free technology to spoil your customers and prospects.

# CHAPTER 59

# SPOIL INFLUENTIAL CUSTOMERS IN CREATIVE WAYS

You can't fake or automate being genuinely interested or authentic with your customers. Your true personality and interest level will show through loud and clear no matter what you do to try and fake it. If you aren't genuinely interested in your customers then you should fix that problem first. Maybe you're just in the wrong business.

Earlier in the book I mentioned several irrational habits that you should develop. While all customers are important, it can really pay to spoil the most influential customers that you do business with. For example, you can use twitalyzer.com, klout.com, or twittergrader.com to check the online influence score of any customer that uses Facebook or Twitter. The higher the score, the more influence that customer has. Might it be worth your time to target the most highly influential customers with special offers and incentives? I'm predicting an entire emerging industry of services and tools that will enable businesses to do just such targeting. Am I telling you to treat some customers better than other customers? If you are smart you will! This does not mean you treat any customers badly, but your top customers are more connected and influential than ever before, so they can be spoiled unlike ever before because of the high likelihood that they will help you spread the word and grow your business as a result.

## IMAGINE THIS SCENARIO

You own a sandwich shop that serves downtown business professionals daily. A sign on the wall encourages your customers to send a quick Twitter message about your business in order to receive a free dessert, or $3 coupon after they are finished. They just show the tweet to any staff member to get the deal.

Several customers participate daily in tweeting a message that gives you free publicity—but it doesn't stop there. A software tool is set up to monitor all of these Twitter messages that mention your sandwich shop, and the tool automatically identifies the most influential customers that send a message (i.e. those with the greatest local following and greatest local influence).

The store manager receives a real-time report of the most socially influential customers that have visited the sandwich shop. At times he can even go out and meet these "VIPs" while they are still in the store.

After a few weeks of tracking, five loyal and very influential customers are identified. The store owner contacts these five customers and tells them that he would like to add a sandwich to the menu for the next three months that is named after these customers. All you ask in return is that these customers share their newfound fame with their followers on Twitter or Facebook.

That's just one idea of dozens more that could be brainstormed. The marketing potential is enormous, and the tools to make it all happen are already here. For example, KLOUT.com makes it easy to see the social influence score of everyone on Twitter.

On the resource page for this book I list services and products that can help you identify your most influential customers and then set about spoiling them or partnering with them in unique ways.

# CHAPTER 60

# REMINDERS PUT MONEY IN THE BANK

**W**e've all heard the statistics. It is far easier to sell something to an existing customer than it is to gain a new customer. If you aren't in the habit of touching base with past customers on a regular basis then you need to implement a strategy for doing so. It's even easier to bring old customers back than it is to get new customers.

If I have an opportunity to spend just five minutes advising a business client on how to most effectively make a bunch of sales quickly, the best advice I can possibly give them is to run some sort of campaign contacting all of their past customers with a special offer.

The tools and technology available to us today make staying in touch far easier than it's ever been before. Here are some examples of how you can easily and automatically stay in touch and remind customers of significant events or dates:

- Send e-mail reminders on important anniversaries, such as one month, six months, or one year after an important purchase. Marketing with e-mail is super-efficient and inexpensive. For more information on automating your e-mail efforts see Part 13 of this book.
- Use a card-sending service, such as sendoutcards.com to automate the process of sending personalized, unique reminder cards, birthday cards, and so on. Check the resource page for details.
- Use Facebook.com and assign someone the task of sending birthday greetings or even a coupon on the birthday of your fans on Facebook.
- So few people today send handwritten notes. This presents you with a huge opportunity to stand out from the crowd. If you take the time to drop three to five thank you notes in the mail every week it will likely

revolutionize your business and your life. The best kind of reminder for people to get is a reminder of how much you appreciate them and value their business, partnership, or friendship.

Don't expect your customers to remember who you are unless you are making frequent efforts to send them timely or heartfelt messages and reminders.

# CHAPTER 61

# REAL-TIME PROBLEM SOLVING *IS* MARKETING

**Y**our business should be in the habit of providing speedy and over-the-top solutions to the issues and concerns that customers bring to your attention. This topic probably could be included in Chapter 6, where I discussed the irrational habits that you should have when dealing with customers, but the discussion about fixing problems fast belongs in this part of the book as well.

The instant a customer has a problem with your service or business there is an imaginary stopwatch that starts ticking. If you wait too long to respond with empathy and a real solution, the odds are against you and the punishment for you could be severe. If a customer detects a lack of attention on your part, they are far more likely to leave a complaint somewhere where many other people will see it. If, on the other hand, you are continually asking your customers how you are doing, you will be the first one to hear when there's an issue. This will give you an opportunity to provide great solutions in a timely fashion before any public complaints have a chance to take root.

An over-the-top satisfied customer can be created from these close-call disasters. These customers can become the best source of testimonials as well. The next time you have a customer service close call, and then go over the top to respond and fix the issue, you should request that the customer put in writing their perspective of the situation. If they give you a glowing review, you've just gotten your hands on some valuable marketing material!

A complaining customer is a very valuable opportunity for any business. You can turn the issue into a case study that illustrates how seriously you take customer service. Some of the best customer service stories start out as potential disasters, but always end with an over-the-top gesture of phenomenal service. Even if you lose a little bit of money or are inconvenienced, it will always be worth it to ensure that customer issues are resolved quickly. Better yet, you could gain a new story that shows the heart of what your business is all about.

Keep in mind that all of your customers now have a megaphone with dozens, hundreds, or possibly even thousands of people listening to whatever they have to say about anything.

In my own business I had an opportunity to apply this principle with a rather large customer transaction. A high-end coaching student of mine who had paid significant money to go through my program had suddenly dropped off the map. He couldn't be contacted and he didn't check in. The generous refund policy that we had in place for the program had more than expired several months before we finally heard from him with a refund request. It would have been very easy for us to deny his refund request on the grounds that we hadn't heard from him in a very long time and that he hadn't attempted to complete the program by even checking in or contacting us. It would have been easy to disappoint the customer, keep the money, and part ways knowing that he had no ground to stand on. Instead I made several personal contacts with the customer asking him how he was doing and, of course, we issued a refund without him having to ask twice. We took the time to be concerned and found out that a death in his immediate family was the cause of his loss of interest in the program. This customer has gone on to be one of my biggest advocates and fans, and continues to do business with us to this day as a result. Had we denied him the refund and not bothered hearing the circumstances, he easily could have gone online and complained. Potentially thousands of dollars of damage to our reputation and future business prospects would have resulted and, worse yet, the true heart of our business would have been misrepresented because our concern for him as a person was always the first priority.

Having encounters such as this to share with new customers is a great way to build their confidence in your organization and help prospects see the heart of what you are all about.

# CHAPTER 62

# PUT GREETING CARDS ON AUTOPILOT

Everyone likes to get personalized mail. I think most business owners have probably had the thought at one time or another that they should have some sort of personal greeting card service running in order to help them stay in touch with their partners, prospects, and customers.

But who has time?

It has never been easier to automate the process of sending cards to those that you know you should be staying in touch with. In much the same way that you can automatically send a series of e-mail messages spread out over time (see Part 13 about e-mail automation), you can also do the same thing with greeting cards. A good card service will also allow you to drop in the mail a fully customized, spur-of-the-moment card with your handwriting inside it. You can do all this *without* touching pens, stamps, or envelopes. By making the card you send out informal, fun, or even humorous you can establish a great deal of rapport with those that you are sending cards to.

One of the people that is better at this than anyone I know is David Frey. I've learned a great deal from him about automating my own greeting card efforts while maintaining a strong personal touch inside each card. I have no idea how many people David stays in touch with this way, but barely a month goes by without him sending me a personal card of some sort with a funny or timely word of encouragement inside it. I have a link on the resource page if you're interested in learning more about working with David and I on automating your greeting card efforts while maintaining a personal touch inside each card.

## CHAPTER 63

# GIVE YOUR CUSTOMERS A VOICE TO BUILD LOYALTY

**W**hile not all business models lend themselves to the concept of social interaction online, many businesses could be taking advantage of this huge opportunity at virtually no expense whatsoever.

Setting up a Facebook fan page or a simple WordPress blog is a fairly straightforward process for any marginally experienced Internet user. Encouraging your customers to stop by your page and post their thoughts or ideas is a great way to build the types of relationships that can only happen with repeated interactions. If a customer feels like they have a voice or some say in the direction of your business, many of them will be far more likely to offer you their thoughts and opinions online rather than in person or on a comment card.

We all like to do business with people that we feel connected to. Open and honest conversations are a great way to establish this type of rapport. But, how can a busy business owner possibly have the time to maintain the multiple relationships that this sort of connection effort will require? Is it possible to allow your customers to speak their minds openly in a public forum and not have it backfire? Isn't it just better to work with customers one at a time and keep them separated?

While there are several legitimate concerns and questions surrounding the idea of having an open forum for customers to gather in an online forum, the potential benefits far outweigh the small expense and time commitment involved in launching such an effort.

Give your customers a voice, listen to them, interact with them, and your business will certainly benefit.

As evidence of this fact, consider a conversation I had with Tim Kerber, the owner of MemberGate software. Tim's software is used by company and membership-site owners around the world to manage membership-based websites (including a site run by Zappos that teaches its customer service methodology to site members). Tim candidly explained to me that there is one common ingredient among the membership websites that thrive, and this same ingredient is typically missing from the membership websites that struggle. That one common element is an active online discussion area where members feel like they can openly share their thoughts and ideas, and have the chance to interact with the owners of the site. I talk more about membership sites in the next chapter.

# CHAPTER 64

# BUILD LOYALTY AND CREDIBILITY WITH A MEMBERSHIP SITE

**O**ne way to strengthen the bond between you and your customers is to have a website established where only those with access privileges are allowed to see all of the content that is stored on the site. These types of sites are called membership sites.

Before you attempt to establish such a site I suggest that you survey your followers or customers and find out what the level of interest is for such a site. If there is significant interest then you can consider pursuing the project. Very few membership websites are successfully established without an already established audience, one that is ready and interested in the topics and content that will be shared on the site.

The membership model has its obvious benefits, but it is not necessarily a simple process to establish a thriving membership site. I currently own and run two separate membership sites that have a total of well over 13,000 members join since they were launched. In my opinion, both sites have had phenomenal success. In this chapter I show you several of the lessons that I've learned from having run these two sites.

A good membership website does not have to cost a lot of money. There are even free WordPress plug-ins that can be used to establish a simple membership site. If you want a more robust solution that includes virtually every conceivable feature, you can invest in a high-end solution such as MemberGate software. Be sure to tell them I sent you if you do go that route. That is the software that I use for both of my membership sites and I've been very happy with how they help run the site behind the scenes.

In my opinion, potential members need to be courted by giving them a lot of very valuable information and content for free in order to help them slowly come to the conclusion that they want to belong to this site and receive the full benefits. On one of our sites we include access to the discussion forum areas at no charge. This allows prospects to see, and actively engage in conversations with, those that are already members. We've found that our current membership ranks make some of our best advocates.

As mentioned earlier, the true lifeblood of any membership site is the discussion forum area. The forum is where members gather and openly discuss issues related to the theme and content of the site. As your site grows, I advise you to reward your most faithful forum members with additional membership benefits, and possibly even a free account, in order to encourage them to continue a high level of activity on the forums.

If you plan to charge your members a recurring fee, such as a monthly, quarterly, or annual member charge, a steady diet of current, relevant, professional content is necessary in order to help members justify the fee. Many of the most successful membership websites that I am aware of have very low monthly fees and deliver loads of great content.

Getting your members involved in the creation of content is a great way to encourage them to buy into the whole concept. The more ownership that your members feel, the more loyal they will be long term.

Some of the easiest and most useful content to add to your site is expert interviews. By encouraging your members to seek out experts in the industry that they would like to see interviewed, you could potentially have a steady stream of great current content ready to deliver to your involved members. I've even trained some of my members on how to conduct a good telephone interview so that they can be fully responsible for acquiring new content. To see my list of interview tips, check out Chapter 93.

# CHAPTER 65

# HOLDING CONTESTS TO BOOST EXPOSURE

**O**nce you have an established account with Facebook, Twitter, or a blog site set up you can begin to run creative contests in order raise the level of interest, loyalty, and awareness among your fans and readers.

For example, I frequently hold contests on my blog where I encourage readers to leave comments and feedback about a blog article that I've recently written and then I randomly pick a winner or several winners for a prize. On occasion I've also invited my readers to vote and choose their favorite or most useful comment left on a blog post. I then award a prize for the winning comment.

On several occasions I've had 200 or more comments left on a blog post as a result of running such contests.

The same type of creative contests can be done on Facebook. I've seen some creative branded T-shirt contests where a significant prize is awarded to the Facebook fan that posts the most unusual picture of themselves on Facebook while using the T-shirt in a creative way.

On Twitter you can hold promotions where you reward followers that reply to your contests or challenges. Since it's possible to have Twitter posts sent to a cell phone via text, your followers don't even have to be online to have a good shot at winning a first-reply-wins type of contest. Alternately, you could have your followers post a promotional phrase to their account during a predetermined time frame and then randomly choose one or more winners from the participants.

In Part 8 of the book I showed some examples of promotions that can be accomplished using cell phones and smartphones.

# PART 16

# POWERFUL MARKETING PARTNERSHIPS

**O**ne of the advantages of being an entrepreneur at this time is the fact that our prospects are gathering in easy-to-access groups or communities at an ever-increasing rate.

It's as if each entrepreneur is a fisherman in a land where new streams and lakes full of fish just keep appearing out of thin air.

The only barrier to accessing these new sources of prospects is our ability to creatively partner with those that own and manage the streams and lakes that we would like to access.

In the following chapters I show you some of the ways that I've successfully partnered with those that manage the sources of prospects that I would like to access. This can be done without spending any money.

# CHAPTER 66

# SET UP A THREE-WAY WIN FOR AN INSTANT BOOST

If I had to identify the one concept that has played the greatest role in my success online it would be the idea of a three-way win. You've heard of win/win arrangements before, but I add a third winner to my strategy when it comes to building a quality e-mail list fast, or getting my message of any kind in front of an entirely new audience. By adding in this third winner I can then actively seek out win/win/win opportunities. By doing this I have built a virtual online empire.

What is win/win/win?

The win/win/win strategy is easily grasped once you are made aware of the virtually infinite number of new communities and influential leaders that there are online. By partnering with these online leaders you can do big things fast. Many businesses are starting to hire affiliate managers just to manage their relationships with powerful online influencers because they recognize that these influential leaders hold the keys to rapid exposure online.

Who are these online influential leaders and where are their communities?

If you don't fully grasp the answer to that question then you need to recognize that the world now has infinitely more communities than ever before in human history. Fifty years ago a community was defined as all of the people that lived within a certain vicinity of each other. For the most part, until recently, geography defined communities. On a Friday night it was common for everyone to attend local high school sporting events and you knew the people that lived near you better than those that didn't.

Now community is defined by infinitely more invisible boundaries. There are communities being built on virtually every imaginable concept, and each of us belong to dozens or hundreds of these communities without even realizing it at times. We add more communities to our lives almost daily. More importantly, the Internet makes it possible for us to gather together in these virtual communities online. This has created a whole new power class of online superstars. These superstars are the influential owners or leaders of these various communities.

There are channel partners who serve the same targeted niche market you do, and even businesses that overlap slightly with yours (but not entirely), and both present partnership opportunities.

Once you grasp the idea of infinite communities, I can easily define what I mean by win/win/win.

### The three parties that must win are:
**A.** The community (otherwise known as the readers, the subscribers, the members, etc.)

**B.** The community leader (the person with influence, the blog owner, the list owner, the person with the popular website). For this example let's assume it's someone with a large targeted e-mail list.

**C.** YOU (the person with great information to share who wants more visitors, traffic, and eyeballs on his stuff)

### The rules of the win/win/win game:
- As long as the community (A) is getting timely, relevant information from their trusted leader (B), they will remain loyal to that source and they will tell others about it in a viral fashion.
- Very few community leaders (B) are so convinced of their own importance as to think only their ideas are good enough to share with their community (A). This opens the door for other experts and content contributors (C) to get in front of the community with the blessing of the leader (B). Most forward-looking community leaders (B) actively seek out top-notch contributors (C) to help keep their community happy, and their own reputation intact.
- A good win/win/win makes the community leader (B) look great and helps him grow his audience. It also makes the community (A) very happy and gives them something they want, and gains YOU (C) the exposure you are seeking. If you can accomplish this sequence successfully even a handful of times, you'll have tremendous success online.
- A good community leader (B) always acts as a filter to keep bad content out (the invisible 90 percent of the job) and let the best content in, so the experience of his loyal community members (A) is protected and strengthened. I've heard this role described as being a curator of content.

- As a content contributor (C) you should *only* work with trusted community managers that have the best interests of their community (A) in mind. Don't do a partnership with anyone that treats their community abusively because your reputation will be tarnished as they eventually go down in flames for abusing their influential position. I've seen it happen many times.
- The best content contributors come from a place of experience, success, motivation, originality, and credibility. To the degree that you lack any of those characteristics it will be harder for you to succeed. If you have all or even some of those character qualities you'll quickly move from a (C) to a trusted and respected (B). Once you are an influential leader to some degree on your own, you will then find it easier to initiate win/win/win arrangements.
- The better the community leader (B) is at managing his community (A) and the larger the community is, the harder it is for you (C) to get your foot in as a contributor, but it's always worth it in the end. I've had potential partners pursue me for months attempting to get some exposure to my 100,000+ e-mail followers. I turn away most people trying to partner with me though.

What are some examples?

You can see the win/win/win strategy played out just by following my free newsletter or blog. While I do write most of the content, I will occasionally offer up content from guest writers that have contacted me, or those with a fantastic relevant product to offer. The guest writers or product owners get exposure and sales, I get commissions and kudos from readers, and the readers get the content they want. As long as I make sure that I filter the content diligently the win/win/win continues.

My first simple e-book I wrote earned me $600 and about 150 subscribers to my e-mail list on the *first day* I launched it. This was well *before* I had any audience of my own. I simply found an e-mail list owner that had an audience made up of people that I thought might be interested in my book. I offered a 50 percent cut (an affiliate commission) on all sales made and asked the list owner to send an informational promotion of my book to her e-mail list. This resulted in several sales and also helped launch my online e-book career. I did the same thing multiple more times with other influential leaders in my niche until I had a well-established following of my own.

If you haven't read the part of the book about using e-mail marketing, check it out in Part 13.

# CHAPTER 67

# LEVERAGE THE POWER OF JOINT VENTURES

The foundation of much of my early success online came as a result of doing joint ventures with other marketers and websites that were servicing my same customer demographic.

These partners agreed to promote my products, articles, and services to their customer base if I would do the same thing for them in return. Over time I've become much more discretionary about who I will enter into such arrangements with. Just because someone is willing to promote my product does not mean I'll be willing to promote theirs. This is because I've learned to protect my audience from any products or information that doesn't resonate with my core principles and message.

If I can find other experts that have a good reputation and high-quality products, I'm very willing to enter into a joint venture partnership with them. If it isn't obvious already, the best way to position yourself for success with joint ventures is to have a large loyal audience. In Internet marketing circles a common phrase is, "He who has the list wins."

In my opinion one of the greatest indicators of marketing prowess is a large, loyal e-mail list of followers that are eager to hear from the owner of that list. There is no stronger position to be in. Find creative ways to partner with these leaders and prosper from it!

# CHAPTER 68

# FIND GOOD PARTNERS FOR MARKETING SYNERGY

$1 + 1 = 3$: Synergy.

Some of the best advice that I got early on in my business career was to be very careful about who I partner with. That advice is still very true, but in the Internet age we live in, there are multiple kinds of partnerships that didn't exist before. These new kinds of partnerships present a whole new level of risk and opportunity.

Ten years ago, entering into a business partnership implied a much stronger, and legally binding arrangement that was full of risks and involved a great deal of planning, lawyers, financial considerations, and so on.

However, when I talk about partnerships in this chapter I'm referring to a much less structured type of arrangement. For example, in previous chapters I talked about joint venture partners, and "three-way win" partners. Some of these partnerships are entered into with only a few minutes of research and negotiation involved, and the partnership activity lasts only a few days. In other cases longer-term partnerships are formed, but in nearly all cases there is a casual and speedy process of compatibility evaluation and agreement on the terms. Nothing is signed, reputations are the handshake, and business goes forward rapidly.

Those who abuse this simple unwritten system go down in flames so quickly that there is a built-in incentive to carefully guard your reputation.

If you recall, in the introduction to this book I talked about the partner that I share a 50/50 arrangement with on our 9,000-member-strong membership website. Andrew Cavanagh and I have never actually met or spoken because we live on opposite sides of the planet. We manage hundreds of thousands of dollars in membership fees and other income annually from our partnership efforts, yet the entire arrangement for our partnership happened in a series of short e-mails exchanged over the course of a couple days over three years ago.

How is such an arrangement possible?

When I approached Andrew initially, he and I both quickly researched the online reputation and accomplishments of the other party, and it was quickly obvious that the combined skill sets and assets that we brought to the table would produce a great deal of synergy and success. In other words, we knew we'd be successful before we even started. It was just a matter of putting the pieces into place.

Those of us that recognize the power of a strong online reputation now have an advantage over everyone else. A bad reputation stands out online easily. Having no reputation stands out almost as glaringly. Having a great reputation, however, is impossible to fake. By establishing your own great reputation and then seeking out simple, complementary partnerships with others that have also built a strong online presence and reputation, you can find amazing partners very quickly. Starting your search can be as simple as spending a few minutes searching online using your industry keywords and Google.

## CHAPTER 69

# BRING DOWN THE BARRIERS BETWEEN YOU AND A GREAT PARTNER

Entering into successful marketing partnerships has never been easier, however you still have to find ways to break the ice and get a conversation started. Everyone is busy, but the only people worth working with are the busy ones.

Most of the most influential people online are very difficult to pin down. They are busy, they have more opportunities than they can possibly tackle, and they don't have a lot of time to consider long-winded proposals. Over the past few years I found myself on this side of the fence after having spent a lot of time in the past trying to pursue those on this side of the fence.

Increased influence for me has meant I've had to ignore many ideas (many of which are fantastic I'm sure) that potential partners have sent me.

So the big question is, how do you get the attention of someone that has a large audience? How do you break down the barrier that separates you from those influential leaders that could benefit from your idea?

Everyone likes to hear from people that make them look good. Even kings and presidents never tire of hearing positive, genuine praise from those that they are surrounded by. It may sound like vanity to some, but from a business perspective, there are few strategies more powerful for getting the attention of a heavy hitter.

Drop a handwritten heartfelt letter of admiration and thanks to someone who's had a positive influence on you. You'll be amazed by the doors that this will open. With the hundreds of proposals that I've gotten in the last several years I could easily recall the small handful of heartfelt, handwritten letters of gratitude.

It may not be easy to hook a big fish to partner with you. Don't get discouraged. Synergy can still happen with less influential partners. Find like-minded individuals with similar levels of influence and partner with them. The synergy will make you rise in the ranks together and before long you will be the one being sought out.

# CHAPTER 70

# Put Your Best Salesmen to Work on Straight Commission

**I**'ve told multiple businesses the same thing: "You'll never again be your own best salesman. Learn to embrace that."

Who is better at selling *you* than you are?

## Your Happy Customers Sell You!

Your social circle of influence, your partners, your customer reviews and testimonials are all far better at selling you and your business than you will ever be, so maybe it's time to stop trying so hard to sell and it's time to start equipping those that like you with the tools that they need in order to sell for you.

Many businesses ignore the fact that their current loyal base of customers is a great source of new business. The best way to put this knowledgeable crowd to work is for you to put into place an incentive program that encourages your current customers to help spread the word about your business. In many cases you don't even need a fancy tracking system. Simply giving your best customers business cards that they can write their name on the back of and pass out to friends will likely suffice. Be generous in offering incentives and prizes to customers that go through the trouble of sending you new business.

The landlords who I use for my business offices offer a referral fee to existing tenants who refer new clients to them. Giving busy professionals a little monetary incentive has helped them add many new tenants and they didn't have to spend any money on advertising in order to make it happen. It's 100 percent pay-for-performance.

### Your Affiliates Are Better at Selling You as Well!

Give your fans (or anyone else who's looking to profit by selling you) more than a pat on the back for bringing you business. Find ways to incentivize and reward those that bring you new business. If possible, automate it and put it all online.

There are even total strangers that are just waiting to help you promote your ideas and products online. These are professional affiliates.

Professional affiliates spend sleepless nights trying to find new ways to drive traffic to offers that will put more money in their pocket. The great thing is, you don't have to pay these affiliates a dime until they make a sale (or bring you a lead, depending on how you are set up). No matter how you get new leads, there are creative marketers in the world just waiting to be given an incentive to drive you qualified traffic. New services are even popping up to enable the payment of affiliates for leads that come from phone calls!

The concept of affiliate marketing first became mainstream online when Amazon.com began offering a small payout to anyone that referred buying traffic to their website. An entire industry soon emerged around affiliate marketers. There are now training courses, conferences, books, and experts all over the world teaching online entrepreneurs how to become professional affiliate marketers. In my opinion, being a professional affiliate marketer is a very difficult way to make a living, but your business can certainly benefit from the millions of online affiliates that are constantly honing their ability to drive traffic to targeted offers and websites.

By offering an affiliate program for your products or services you are, in effect, hiring potentially hundreds or thousands of commission-only sales people who work relentlessly to send you new customers. The good news is they are only paid for results, not for time spent working for you.

Since several of my business models include selling information and digital goods, I can afford to offer commissions of 50 percent or more on all sales to the affiliate marketers that refer traffic to me. The majority of the new customers that I get in any given month are a result of my network of thousands of affiliates referring steady streams of new traffic to me in the hopes that a sale will be made and they will earn a commission for it. In my case the entire process is managed by Clickbank.com. Clickbank helps assign affiliate links to each of my products, tracks each sale, processes the orders, ensures I get paid, and that affiliates get paid the share they've been promised. It's a booming business with thousands of vendors (the authors or owners of content, courses, downloads, or even traditional books) and hundreds of thousands of affiliates who are constantly building websites, writing articles, launching blogs, and doing e-mail marketing campaigns, all aimed at selling the products that other vendors have created. In nearly all cases, when an affiliate makes a sale for me I have no idea who they are, where they live, or how they sent me traffic, but I'm always grateful for the new customer, and I'm always happy to see them get paid their commissions automatically via Clickbank.

Even if you aren't in a business where information or downloadable goods are being sold, you still should be able to benefit from having an affiliate program. Companies like CJ.com are set up to assist all types of businesses with their affiliate marketing efforts.

> The primary benefit of having an affiliate program is that you are allowing any number of new online salespeople to start promoting your products and services far and wide online, and they only get paid based on performance.

### Your Online Reputation Is a Salesman, Too!

I spent a lot of time early in the book addressing online reputation management and enhancement. Efforts spent managing that aspect of your business is a fantastic marketing strategy. Your reputation can become your best salesman and you don't even have to pay a commission.

# CHAPTER 71

# CROSS PROMOTIONS ARE MARKETING SYNERGY

**I**f you can identify the other businesses that service a similar demographic as your business then you've likely found a good candidate for a cross promotion. It's especially easy to set up such promotions if both parties have a similar size audience. A cross promotion occurs when you each agree to send out a promotion supporting the other party's business.

Online these types of arrangements happen frequently. If both parties use an affiliate link to track the number of sales and pay the other party an agreed-on commission, you eliminate any concerns over the two of you having different size audiences or differing response rates to the offers.

I've helped dozens of new online marketers get established by promoting their quality products to my audience. This grows their e-mail list, gives my customers the quality products and information they want, and earns me commissions on the products I promote.

# CHAPTER 72

# USE GUEST ARTICLE SWAPS FOR EASY EXPOSURE TO TARGETED AUDIENCES

**O**nce you've identified potential partners that are serving a similar target niche you can do article swaps with them to help spread your message. Blog swaps or newsletter article swaps allow both of you to gain exposure that you otherwise would not have had. Often industry-specific blogs are open to guest articles as well.

Even if the other list owner or blog owner isn't interested in sending you an article in exchange, you'll find that many are open to posting your article simply to provide their readers with quality content. You won't know until you ask!

Don't just look for blogs in your niche. Try to find markets that serve on the edges of your market, but that serve a similar demographic. For example, I've found that real estate investors tend to respond very positively to my Internet marketing advice articles—even when I have no mention of real estate in the article.

When you guest post, ask permission to insert limited links into your article. Don't overdo it. No one wants to load up their blog or website with links sending readers running away.

Reassure your blog host that you will be promoting the article to your reader base once it is posted on their site. This is a great way to return the favor for their kindness.

# CHAPTER 73

# EXPERT INTERVIEWS: SIMPLE AND POWERFUL MARKETING CONTENT

**E**veryone enjoys being considered an expert by their peers. Use this universal truth to your advantage. Most experts in any field will readily agree to being interviewed by an engaging fellow expert with a win–win proposition.

Some of the easiest and most potent content that you can ever deliver to your audience will simply be interviews with relevant experts.

If you find yourself having trouble getting the attention of the higher-level experts in your field, then I suggest you use what I call *the bottom-up approach*. When using the bottom-up approach to secure experts, you start by contacting the least influential and most eager experts in your field of interest. For example, these are the authors that appear well beyond page one on Amazon.com or Google.com. These experts aren't hard to find and typically they are more than willing to volunteer the information they know in a telephone interview regardless of your marketing power or intentions. Once you've approached and interviewed several of the lesser-known experts you can begin to approach the more influential experts with a bit more credibility and experience, and you'll find that most of them will be far more likely to agree to an interview if you've already interviewed people that they consider to be their peers. Of course, you will have gotten testimonials from each of them as well!

More influential experts may be interested in knowing what your marketing plans are in exchange for their valuable ideas and time. The best answer you can give them is that you'll be exposing them to your large following. Ideally, this is a large e-mail list, a popular blog, or another popular forum.

**Figure 73.1**

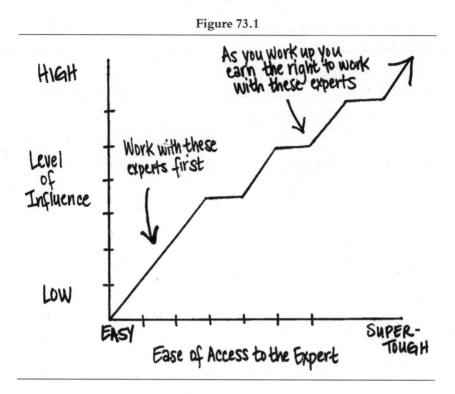

What if you don't have an audience yourself yet to help convince the big fish that you are worth the effort?

The bottom-up strategy still works. It may take slightly more effort, but when approaching experts who are lower on the totem pole you can suggest to them that you will provide them with a copy of your interview, as well as a full transcript, for their use in whatever way they see fit for their own audience. Inside the transcript that you create you can include links back to your blog or, better yet, your e-mail list. As your list grows so does your ability to attract influential leaders in your niche.

As you work your way up the totem pole of influential people in your niche (see Figure 73.1), you will find it easier and easier to get the time and attention of both the experts and the audiences that they are reaching. With each interview you conduct, be sure to deliver the content of the interview in an attractive, professional format that the experts can easily share with their own audience. If you conduct a high energy, exciting, personal, and engaging interview the expert will be more than delighted to share it with their audience. Most people have no problem with you conservatively sprinkling in your contact information, your website, or details on joining your e-mail list.

There are several free tools you can use to accommodate such interviews. I've frequently used the services of freeconferencecall.com to conduct interviews by phone and then easily generate an MP3 or WAV file for easy distribution to my audience.

Transcription services such as internettranscribers.com can be used to turn any spoken recording into a written transcript. The services I use also are able to correct the grammar as they create the document because few of us speak in full sentences.

An attractive e-cover can easily be created, as well as using any number of e-book or e-cover services online.

Give the file, the transcript, and the attractive cover to every expert you interview and request that they give the product away as a download to their followers (or sell the product and keep the proceeds). Of course, inside of the product will be a handful of conservative references to you and instructions on joining your e-mail list or getting more information from you.

See Chapter 93 for some great tips for interviewing experts (or anyone else for that matter).

## CHAPTER 74

# RECOGNIZE TOP SERVICES WITH A TESTIMONIAL FOR UNEXPECTED REWARDS

**S**ome of the best marketing partners you can have are the businesses and services you rely on to help you run your business. They can be a great source of referral business, exposure, and back links for your website.

For example, I've been a fan of aweber.com for a long time because they help me manage my e-mail marketing efforts with excellence. I sent them a nice testimonial several years ago, and to this day they still have it posted on their site along with a link pointing back to my website. I've had thousands of visitors to my site as a result of that one link.

If I ever read a great article online, or a useful blog post, I'm always sure to leave a comment or send an e-mail expressing my appreciation. I also give them permission to use my comments for promotional purposes as they see fit. By doing this I'm helping them out while they help me out.

## PART 17

# MAKE YOUR
# STORY POWERFUL

**W**hat's the story behind your business? Every entrepreneur loves answering that question, and most prospects and customers love hearing the answer, but very few businesses ever capitalize on these two facts.

Knowing the story behind your business, and knowing how to make that story include your customer is vital to your overall marketing message.

# CHAPTER 75

# DOCUMENT THE STORY OF YOUR BUSINESS

**B**y now you've probably heard someone besides me talk about the power of your story as a marketing tool.

While it may feel a bit like old news to encourage you to work on your story, nonetheless, having one is a marketing essential. The best marketing stories aren't just a retelling of the history of your business. No one really cares how long you've been in business or even how many family generations it's been passed through. That may sound a bit harsh, but keep in mind that your prospect is asking, "What's in it for me?" not, "How long have you been in business?"

Incorporating your ideal customer and your proven ability to over-deliver to that ideal customer is essential. Think back to some of your earliest success stories with some of those perfect-fit customers. Include the impact you had on them as part of your story. Post your story on your website or blog where it is easily accessed and educate all employees to reflect the core values of your story.

If done correctly your story will become a distinguishing and brand-building badge that captures who you are, what you are good at, and provide evidence of it.

If you are struggling to capture your story in a way that you find engaging and useful, try interviewing a few of your top customers for inspiration. What was it about your business that first attracted them? How are you doing compared to the other options out there? What impact has working with you had on them?

Your story isn't written once and abandoned. Make each new prospect aware of how they help you continue the story.

It will require you to know your audience well. Who are your target customers? That's whom the story is for.

## Sell Your *Why*

Part of your story needs to be the *why* behind your business.

Why do you do what you do? By incorporating the why into your marketing efforts, you are inviting people to emotionally attach to the bigger cause behind your business efforts.

I believe that my success in online business is directly tied to my willingness to share with my customers the why behind what I do. Most businesses never identify, or don't have, a why behind their business and, even if they do know why they do what they do, most businesses don't share it with the rest of us.

It's time to expose the why of your business.

The why of your story can't simply be profits (although that's certainly necessary to stay in business). The bigger why will get you increased loyalty and exposure that up until now has been nearly impossible to achieve.

Here's how it works:

We know that your customers organize online in groups that all have common life passions and interests. If the why behind your business resonates with a few influential and connected customers, you could find yourself being touted by some big hitters who buy into your big vision.

**Some examples I've seen myself:**
- An online general-merchandise seller who seeks to employ inner-city youth and help them learn life skills (see this book's Foreword).
- A tech company that actively shares its technology to help end world hunger.
- A restaurant that launched a clothing line aimed at helping control the pet population.
- A business (mine) that tries to help parents earn an income from home so their children can have maximum exposure and influence from Mom and Dad.

While not every prospect will necessarily agree with the principles or worldview of your "why," the vast majority of customers appreciate knowing the true driving force behind any business they are working with. In my experience, the number of customers that will become passionately interested in your business as a result of understanding your bigger purpose will far offset any customers that decide not to do business with you as a result of you revealing your bigger purpose.

For example, I love to teach anyone that will listen about the strategies and tools that are available to them to help them succeed on the Internet. I feel a special affinity, though, for parents who are trying to establish an income from home, so they can be more of the parent that they'd like to be. It's not that my ideas work better for parents, but by simply revealing my core passion to help parents, I have earned a greater degree of loyalty and respect from those in my audience that are parents. On the occasion that I have non-parents, such as bachelors or retirees, attending my training, I've yet to have any of them complain when I express my passion for helping parents.

The fact is, I'm not too concerned about whether someone agrees with the why behind my business efforts. Revealing my core values is part of being authentic. If I can't do what I do while being authentic, then I should reexamine the way I am spending my life.

Write down the story of the why behind your business and share it with your core customers when the opportunity presents itself. This is a great topic of discussion for social media platforms, or for e-mail marketing messages.

In Chapter 86 I have more ideas that might help you tell your story.

# CHAPTER 76

# CREATE YOUR UNIQUE SELLING PROPOSITION (USP) BASED ON YOUR STORY

**B**y shaping your story and sharing what makes you unique among your competitors, you begin to create an overall marketing message that simply cannot be competed with.

Without even realizing it, I accomplished this with one of the first simple e-books that I wrote. It was a book about my success story using eBay in a creative way. It was about 10 years ago, when eBay was first starting to become mainstream. There were literally hundreds of books on the subject of using and selling on eBay. Had I done any research on exactly how many other books there were on the subject, I might've been discouraged and become convinced that I shouldn't stray into such a crowded niche market, but I was bold or foolish enough to proceed anyway.

Fortunately for me I built the story of the book (and the sales copy for the book) around my own personal success on eBay. In other words, the book showed others exactly how I did what I did. While I wasn't the only one doing things this way, I was the only one willing to share that information with others in a creative way.

Because I was willing to be transparent in the way that I ran my business, and because I was willing to share my secrets, my book easily stood apart from all of the other books about eBay—most of which were about as entertaining as reading the eBay.com help menu.

To this day I'm pretty sure that I have the all-time best-selling book about how to succeed on eBay. I can easily track my success back to the fact that I was willing to tell my story instead of simply creating another how-to guide.

In order for your story to become your USP (Unique Selling Proposition) I believe you must include your customer in the story somehow. Make the customer feel like your story isn't complete until you add them into it. In my case my book promised to show each reader how they could learn to see eBay in the same creative way I did, and then we'd partner together with other readers and share creative ideas that benefited all of us that got it. That's exactly what my first membership website consisted of—thousands of people who had read and loved my book. My story is still being written and it includes all of my valued customers. I think it worked especially well because I created an active and thriving online community around my niche.

# PART 18

# ACTUALLY, YOU ARE SELLING *YOU*

I believe that we are entering into a new era of customer expectations. Fewer and fewer people are willing to be sold anything. Prospects are still buying things to be sure, but the resistance to being sold anything has never been higher. Just ask any car salesman that has been in the business for more than 15 years or so about the changes that he perceives. Customers used to walk into a car showroom and seek out the most knowledgeable sales rep so that they could educate themselves on the features and benefits of the different vehicles. Today customers walk in knowing as much, if not more, about the vehicles than the car salesmen themselves.

The only way to distinguish yourself in an environment where prospects are already hypereducated is to be the most helpful and authentic company and individual that you can be. Facts are no longer closely guarded secrets that can be used to impress your customers. Facts are instantly available on Google and freely distributed.

The easiest way to be truly authentic is to recall the old Sunday school lesson of putting others before yourself. If you truly keep the best interests of your customers and prospects in mind when dealing with them, you will be rewarded both financially and with the knowledge that you have been truly authentic and helpful in your business efforts.

After that, get comfortable sharing online the stuff that makes you who you are. You don't have to expect everyone to agree with you or like your choices, but being *authentic* goes a long way towards establishing trust. The people in my industry who share the most about their personal lives, families, trips, troubles, and failures online are the ones that attract the most loyal and raving fans.

The only thing left to sell is *you*. What makes you different and important? You'd better find out fast if you don't know, because the world is eagerly awaiting your answer.

## CHAPTER 77

# WHEN USING HUMOR IN YOUR MARKETING, BE SURE TO LAUGH AT YOURSELF

*Laughing at our mistakes can lengthen our own life. Laughing at someone else's can shorten it.*

—Cullen Hightower

Incorporating humor into your marketing is a great way to connect while telling a story. You should proceed with caution though!

Most good jokes run the risk of offending someone, yet humor is vital to your success as a leader and influencer. What's the solution?

I've heard it said on several occasions that there's only one type of humor that's always funny and always safe. Poking fun at yourself and your own shortcomings is the best way to use humor to add warmth and engage an audience on- or offline. Simply telling jokes only communicates that you found a good joke book recently. On the other hand, finding creative ways to poke fun at yourself tells people that you are human and that they can relate to you.

You've heard the old saying, "People don't care how much you know until they know how much you care."

I can change that up a bit for this brief chapter: "People don't care how much you know until they know you are willing to poke fun at yourself."

Often on Facebook I post funny family stories or tales of failure on my part. One of the most commented-on posts I ever left on Facebook.com was about my adventure chasing the mail truck down our street in the middle of winter in my socks trying to hand our driver a Christmas card. Each time I'd get close behind her she pulled forward to another house. I looked like a fool doing it, but I shared it all on Facebook and as a result, many of my readers enjoyed a good laugh at my expense while posting witty comments and banter. Those kinds of posts do more for my reputation and relationship with my followers than do five other posts with great content.

If you want to be memorable and come across as genuine be sure to tell the world about your flaws and failures in a lighthearted manner regularly.

This may seem like a simple or obvious lesson, but even the most cutting-edge and social media-savvy companies have struggled to get the humor issue right. Consider one of the most cutting-edge and social savvy websites online, Groupon.com. In late 2010 this coupon and social-media-driven company was nearly bought for $6 billion by Google.com. Obviously they were (and probably still are) doing something very right. Then, in early 2011 Groupon.com took its first stab at television marketing by purchasing expensive ads during the most-watched sporting event of the year, the Super Bowl. The ads were supposed to be humorous and self-deprecating, but instead they lost thousands of users because of how offensive many people found their ads to be. The problem, in my opinion, is the fact that the self-deprecating nature of the ads was not obvious enough for general audiences. It was almost an inside joke and it backfired horribly. Because of the massive and loyal online following that Groupon.com enjoys, it is entirely inexcusable that they ran such ads before testing them with a handful of their most loyal followers.

To get the full extent of the story, do a search on Google for the phrase "Groupon Super Bowl Tibet." Now consider this example, by someone who is living it out and doing it right.

One of my favorite speakers to listen to is Dave Roever (pronounced "reever"). He's a heroic man because he served the United States bravely in Vietnam and suffered some of the most severe burn wounds that you are likely to ever see on an otherwise active and energetic man. These are the types of wounds that could have ended the hopes and dreams of a lesser man, but for decades he's been using his disarming demeanor and the story of his struggles to bring a message of hope and healing to millions of people in churches, public schools, military bases, and countless other forums worldwide. I've heard him speak on multiple occasions and have heard some of the same stories and illustrations on more than one occasion, but I'm still held captive every time, as is everyone else in attendance.

His secret?

I'm sure that one of the key reasons he continues to be such an effective speaker is that he has come to naturally present his flaws, injuries, and struggles in an honest, humorous way whether he's in front of thousands or just in one-on-one conversations with those that need his message most. He's a serious man with a serious mission, but he always finds time to find the humor in his circumstances and obstacles. There's a great lesson for us all in the life of Dave Roever.

# CHAPTER 78

# SHARE YOUR LIFE OPENLY FOR MARKETING AUTHENTICITY

The bar has been raised.

Now more than ever customers and prospects want to know the people behind the businesses they are doing business with.

I made the observation a couple of years ago that a lot of CEOs were starting to appear in television commercials. That was extremely uncommon 15 years ago. It's almost as if all big businesses are now on trial, and they are all trying to convince us that they really are human at their core. Those megacorporations have a difficult challenge in front of them, don't they? How can a billion-dollar company connect with the average guy on Facebook? They are recognizing the same thing we all are: We want to do business with people we know and trust. We want to do business with *people.*

We have it easier as smaller businesses. Just by the nature of our size we are automatically more approachable. If you use the right tools, you can build life-long loyal relationships (yes, even online).

We've all heard the skeptical business people say things like, "I don't need Facebook, I don't care what someone had for breakfast today." A statement like that tells me that they don't quite get it. They will eventually, if they have a cause, a dream, or a business to share.

An essential element of raising the trust level between you and those that your business is trying to attract is authenticity. Perhaps the best way to build a relationship based on authenticity is to openly share and discuss details about your life and who you really are *without* making the conversation about you all the time.

Nearly all of the most successful users of the major social media networks will tell you the same thing. If you try to use social media as an advertising platform, your efforts will likely fail miserably.

If however, you use social networks to connect with your customers in personal ways by discussing issues in much the same way that you might at an informal gathering, then you are likely to see genuine relationships and loyal customers emerge from the process over time.

Don't be the guy that always talks about himself in social settings. Be the guy that asks interesting questions while not being afraid to reveal his own faults and failures. That's being approachable and authentic. The more you begin to share who you really are, the more likely you are to be embraced by those listening to you.

## How Much Is Too Much?

How far should you go with sharing your life details online?

Are religion and politics open topics on your business or personal Facebook or Twitter account?

These are tough questions that everyone is still trying to figure out. Nearly all large businesses have to protect their brand by staying neutral on all things potentially controversial. But even for the smaller businesses or one-man operations there are plenty of experts that will tell you that authenticity doesn't have to mean sharing your feelings about issues like religion or politics. For some people this advice is probably true, but I would disagree that religion and politics are off limits as a rule. Give people some credit for being capable of having a relationship with someone that they don't see eye-to-eye with on all major issues.

Some of us (am I the only one?) are perfectly capable of disagreeing with someone on a political issue, but still doing business with them if they are the best at what they do. I'm not sure I want to get into lifelong customer/business relationships with those that aren't able to think that way. If you find out what church I go to on Sunday, and that makes you want to not do business with me, I'm sure I won't be losing any sleep over losing you as a customer.

Instead of turning people off, I've found that the opposite effect has occurred in many instances. I'm never intentionally controversial, but when I've made mention of my stances on issues of faith or politics, inevitably I'm contacted privately or publicly by a ratio of about 20:1 by people that appreciate it and tell me how much more loyalty they feel because of my willingness to take a stand on important issues. Some people storm off angrily because they aren't capable of hearing anyone with a different opinion. Those kinds of people don't make great customers anyway though, and they aren't missed at all.

The matter of crossing into personal areas is a tough call, and it's a decision you'll have to make on your own, but I don't avoid it. You'll frequently find me asking interesting questions on stories or issues that affect us all. I don't feel the need to try to pretend to be entirely neutral on all of the most controversial issues just because I'm running a business. There is a right time and place for all discussions in my opinion, and I have earned a great deal of respect even from those with different worldviews than mine because I allow them to make their case as well. I love being surrounded by people with strong opinions as opposed to people too afraid to speak. Is it just me that thinks this way?

# CHAPTER 79

# DISTINGUISH YOURSELF AND YOUR BUSINESS WITH THE X FACTOR

**W**hat will really set you and your business apart online or off?

If you had to identify one overriding principle to commit to that you could never compromise on, what would it be?

Even if times got tough, budgets got stretched, and the pressure was really on, what is that core value that would keep you focused even if it meant going down to failure as a business?

For me the answer is the same for all three questions, and I think it should be for your efforts as well. I see it working time and time again in not only business settings, but also in personal affairs.

Before I give my answer, let me walk down memory lane with you for a moment.

I remember when the Internet was first being commonly used as a tool for business in the mid-1990s. There were a great deal of cons and illegitimate businesses set up with anonymous owners hiding in the comfort of their basements (or in many cases their mom's basement). The anything-for-a-dollar crowd was everywhere online. I remember the best advice back then were phrases such as:

- "Don't ever use your credit card online—are you nuts?"
- "You can't believe what you read online!"

Times have changed now, though.

- Billions of trusting customers are doing business with millions of online merchants every day, and both sides are happy with the end result.

- People actually *do* believe what they read online, in most cases well before they'll believe anything in the newspaper or on TV. This is true even for non-Internet related purchases such as restaurant choices or retail shopping. The crowd has figured it out.

How are these trends possible?

Are there fewer scammers? No.

Are people just more trusting in general? No.

Have brilliant laws been passed to make all this possible? Please! That's definitely not it. The cry to politicians from online businesses and consumers is "Please continue to leave us alone!"

The fact is, *we the people* have put systems in place for knowing whom we can and can't trust. It seems we are quite good at it. Internally there is a scale that must be tipped before we'll listen, take advice, connect, or purchase from anyone online. The good guys are rising to the top. Those same good guys also know that all it takes is one false move and the crowd will quickly spread the word about their failure and the established trust will topple like a house of cards.

So, back to my question then: How do you stand out in this environment?

It's not free samples, charisma, the right keywords, or a search-engine-optimized site. All of those things are worthy pursuits in different cases, but there's one overriding character quality that must be adapted in order for you to stand head and shoulders above every other possible option your customers might ever consider.

This is the true X factor of any successful business in my opinion.

Here it is: Put your customer's best interests first no matter the cost.

It's the old Sunday school lesson applied to the Internet: "Do unto others as you'd have them do unto you."

If you want to shine and have a raving fan base, that's the foundation to stand on. Any attempts to fake it or cut corners on that principle will have dire consequences, because every one of your customers has a megaphone and they can ignore you with a mouse-click, or worse yet, they can tell the world how fake you really are.

This is the ultimate free-marketing strategy.

# CHAPTER 80

# SERVING AND MARKETING AT THE SAME TIME

**O**dds are you haven't heard of CleaningForAReason.org yet, but this is a perfect example of serving and marketing at the same time.

Over 800 cleaning companies around the United States and Canada partnered with CleaningForAReason.org to provide free house cleaning for anyone undergoing chemotherapy.

Cleaning companies that have participated in this program have undoubtedly benefited. The money they are losing by providing free services has no doubt been made up for in new clients, positive exposure, and an overall sense of purpose and selflessness in their business. I'd imagine it's also done wonders for morale among the staff.

Even if we assume (falsely, I'm sure) that there are ever-selfish intentions behind such generous efforts, you can't deny the viral marketing impact that such a gesture can potentially have on any business. Good news spreads faster and further than ever. Create good news by serving. It's almost irrational to giveaway so much, but then again, being irrationally generous in your service and approach is something I fully endorse (see Chapter 6).

# CHAPTER 81

# STRATEGICALLY ASKING FOR HELP CAN BE GREAT MARKETING

As children we instinctively ask a lot of questions. If you've been around a three- or four-year-old recently you know exactly what I'm talking about.

For some reason, though, our culture demands that we began asking fewer questions as we "mature." I know that public schools drove that message home quite clearly for me. Only the uncool or slow students asked questions.

The truth is, though, most, if not all, of my successful online businesses have been a result of me asking my customers a lot of questions. Just because I'm the expert does not mean that I know all there is to know about what should be done next, or what products my customers want, or what industry trends everyone should be paying attention to.

Another benefit of asking questions is that you present yourself as being authentic. Nobody likes to hang out with someone that seems to have their ears turned off, but is constantly teaching others new things because they are the expert.

I've noticed a very predictable trend on my Facebook account. My personal Facebook account has about 5,000 friends, which is the current limit for a personal Facebook page. In spite of that fact, there are often times that a comment or post that I make will receive only a small handful of replies. That's okay with me, because I'm not trying to get the maximum number of replies; I'm just trying to share a useful thought or interesting fact. What does surprise me, though, is the response that I get when I ask questions.

Everyone enjoys the feeling of helping someone out, so when I run into a situation where I could use some advice, or the input of my online friends, I don't hesitate to post my question where others can see it and respond.

Of course the greatest benefit of asking your audience questions is that you can let them decide what products and services you will provide next.

Asking questions and opinions of people that you're trying to get to know online is also a great way to establish first contact. For example, I do my best to personally answer any e-mail inquiries that I get (within reason), and often times those who are bold enough to ask good questions eventually wind up being some of my best customers and even partners. You can tell a lot about somebody by what questions he or she asks.

Surveymonkey.com is a great, easy–to-use, free tool that takes surveys of your audience. A simple three or four question survey asking your current customers how you are doing, and what else they would like to see you doing, can reap great rewards. Just knowing that you care enough to ask their opinion will help establish a better relationship, but if you respond to their feedback and suggestions with personal notes and follow-up, you will be taking a huge step toward establishing a very strong relationship with each customer that took the time to respond.

# CHAPTER 82

# BE CONTROVERSIAL TO ATTRACT A CROWD

$\mathbf{B}$y surveying your customers you can likely discover some of the most disturbing and disappointing trends in your industry. Once you are aware of these annoyances and issues, you should choose one (or several depending on the issue), and then go after that issue in defense of your customers. Expose it, purge it from your business, and go after it where it appears anywhere else.

For example, in my industry of teaching people the strategies and tools required for earning money using the Internet, there are a lot of annoyances to go after. For instance, there are many well-meaning experts that use unscrupulous tactics to increase their sales numbers.

Through conversations with my customers, and by observing conversations that are happening on popular chat forums, I've discovered that most people are getting very frustrated by the number of big launches that keep occurring in our industry.

A big launch is when a new course or product by an established expert is hyped for several weeks as being the next fantastic, must-have course. It's enough to drive anyone crazy if you're paying attention to too many experts.

However, it's a fact for me that I could easily make hundreds of thousands of dollars more per year (if not a whole lot more) if I would participate frequently in these big launches. Partners typically earn commissions of 50 percent or more on the sale of all products during such launches. Because of the loyalty and size of my mailing list I could cash out frequently on these big launches, but I chose not to. I also take it a step further in many cases.

In many instances I've picked a fight with those launching overpriced, overhyped courses and I've taken them to task on the way they are treating the customers in our industry. Not only was this the right thing to do, but it has also earned me a great deal of respect and trust among the customers that follow me. It has not earned me a whole lot of new friends in my industry, but there are many that do agree with me, even if they are very supportive only secretly.

These blog posts and articles have been very popular, and inevitably I pick up several new customers (and increase the loyalty of my current customers) each time I take a stand.

# CHAPTER 83

# BECOME INCREASINGLY INDISPENSABLE

As successful marketing strategies become more and more about making personal connections and being authentic, it becomes increasingly important that you insert *yourself* as a vital component of your marketing efforts.

This means using your face, your thoughts, and your opinions on the most important industry or niche trends related to your business. It's time to take a stand on the things that are important to you and to let those positions be known.

Doing this will eventually make you indispensable to your audience, while those that are constantly neutral on all of the controversial issues will more easily be forgotten.

I see a great example of the power of being indispensable with many of my own readers. Whenever a new product or idea is introduced to the market, many of my customers faithfully wait to hear my opinions and insights *before* they will take action and make up their mind. It's not that they aren't capable of choosing on their own, rather they are interested in hearing my thoughts before they feel like they have the full story. That puts me in a position of being indispensable.

If I am unwilling to take a stand on important issues then it is unlikely that my audience will ever consider me indispensable. If you want to be an indispensable part of the decision-making process that your customers are making, then you must be willing to take clear stands both for and against those things you do and don't agree with.

If you can master the fine art of being sharply opinionated without ever being negative, you will quickly become indispensable.

**Other ways to be increasingly indispensable:**

- Be creative. Don't just respond or implement, but *create*.
- Be almost irrationally optimistic. People need the boost, and they'll come to rely on it.
- Be consistently available with a steady stream of great content and ideas that you giveaway at no cost.
- Give positive, solution-based commentary on all trends related to your niche.
- Respond with thorough public replies to the issues being faced by your followers.
- Be available.
- Be transparent.
- Truly have the best interests of your audience at heart.
- Be worthy of being followed online in every imaginable way you can think to apply that term.
- Be controversial and opinionated *without* being negative.

# CHAPTER 84

# BE ACCESSIBLE OR BE IGNORED

One of the old standards by which we measured successful people was how inaccessible they were. The more inaccessible they were, the more successful they seemed to be. This phenomenon just doesn't impress people any longer. No matter how important or successful you are, you better still be available to the prospects and customers who are taking the time to try and connect with you. Better yet, one of the primary tasks of building your business as a leader should be making time regularly to connect at the base level with those people that your business is touching.

Even the largest of corporations are starting to realize that their top decision-makers need to be more in touch with their average prospects and customers. Simply setting up a Facebook or Twitter account with your business name won't be enough—especially if you're a small business. People want to deal with real people, and if they feel like they have access to the top decision-makers, they are far more likely to form a long-term relationship with your company. You need to personally be engaged on Facebook and Twitter in order to be successful with social media.

Don't put layers of obstacles between the leaders of your business and your customers. Maybe this is a chapter that should have gone in the Chapter 6 section about irrational habits, because in the old economy it wasn't as necessary for business owners and leaders to be as in touch with their customer base as it is now.

Being inaccessible now just comes across as being uninterested, or too important to have to deal with the real people that are your prospects and customers.

# CHAPTER 85

# THE PASSIONATE, GENEROUS ARTIST IN ALL OF US MUST BE RELEASED

**O**ne of the great things about being alive in the time we live in is that excellence is so much easier to share when we encounter it. The best of the best open market ideas rise to the top so much faster than ever before because we are able to spread them virally.

Creativity and passion are recognized and shared much faster than ever before.

We are finally able to reward and spread the word about those remarkable, talented artists that take their craft so seriously that we can't help but tell the world with the social megaphones we all have.

## FROM SETH GODIN'S BOOK *LINCHPIN*:

Do you remember the old American dream?

It struck a chord with millions of people (in the United States and in the rest of the world, too.) Here's how it goes:

- Keep your head down
- Follow instructions
- Show up on time
- Work hard
- Suck it up

. . . you will be rewarded.

As we've seen, that dream is over.

257

The new American dream, though, the one that markets around the world are embracing as fast as they can, is this:

- Be remarkable
- Be generous
- Create art
- Make judgment calls
- Connect people and ideas . . . and we have no choice but to reward you.

It's worth noting that when Seth writes "create art" he doesn't just mean painting or sculpting. I think he's including all passionate, dedicated creative thinkers that take the road less traveled on their way to "making a difference" in any industry.

Is Seth's new American dream an attack on the idea of hard work? Of course not.

It's an encouragement (in my opinion) to make you a revolutionary. Stand out, stand up, and be taken seriously. This isn't something you can simply demand, but if you take the time to be generous and truly care, then I think you'll find an eager audience for whatever your calling is.

Go back and read Chapter 79 if you haven't yet.

# CHAPTER 86

# THE POWER OF YOUR *WHY*

$\mathbf{I}$t may seem strange for a marketing book to include a chapter about your core motivations for doing what you do, but in an age where authenticity and transparency are crucial elements of business success, this chapter belongs here.

The reason I include this chapter is because it has never been more crucial to your success that you be fully sold and convinced that you really are doing what you love to do with your life. I've seen statistics that tell me that upwards of 80 percent of all Americans are in a job that they find at least somewhat unfulfilling. This is a sad statistic.

For those of us doing what we love to do for a living, it is vital that we find creative ways to communicate that message to our prospects and customers. It shouldn't be very hard to do if we actually do love what we do.

Given the choice, customers will always gravitate towards those that obviously love doing what they do. You can't fake this.

## WHAT IF I'M NOT DOING WHAT I LOVE RIGHT NOW?

This book is not intended for those with a working-for-the-weekend mindset, so as long as that's not you, let me give you this encouragement: There has never been a better time in human history to be an entrepreneur. The tools we have available to us, the low barriers to entry, and all of the gender, racial, and religious barriers that have been huge factors in the past have all been tilted as far in your favor as they will ever be thanks to the Internet.

There simply is no excuse to be doing *anything* except what you were made to do. Follow that inner passion. Even if you have to start out doing it part-time, I encourage you to begin using the tools that I've mentioned in this book to establish your own business and begin growing it as you increase your own expertise and leadership skills in your chosen niche. Passionate followers will find passionate leaders. Why can't you be one of those passionate leaders?

# CHAPTER 87

# APPEALING TO
# THE INFLUENTIAL

**B**ecause I am a father of five, I've seen all of the good kid movies of the last decade. In the popular Pixar film *Ratatouille* the setting is a classy restaurant where some serious tensions exist between the cooking and wait staff because of the impending need to really impress the most influential and respected local food critics.

In this movie the restaurant has the advantage of knowing exactly who the food critics are, and they recognize them when they enter the restaurant. They are then able to put their best effort into making sure that the critics have a great experience. That's a bit of an unfair advantage don't you think?

In real life your business typically has no idea who the most influential customers are as they enter and exit your business. This is true if you are doing business online or offline.

Wouldn't it be nice to know how influential each of your customers *really* are? Unfortunately it's still impossible to identify all of these influencers, even with all of the technology we have. There is good news though. By tracking the social influence ranking of your customers, you can start to identify who some of the most socially influential people are in your customer and prospect base.

Sites like Klout.com and TwitterGrader.com can help you identify who the Twitter leaders are among your clients and prospects. You only need capture their Twitter ID and use the information you gather there to your advantage. This is an emerging concept, but I propose that tracking influence and then acting on it will become a mainstream marketing activity. This is your chance to be on the cutting edge.

I'm not advocating that you show favoritism and give bad service to low-influence customers while reserving your good service for important customers. What I am suggesting is that it is now possible to know who some of your most influential customers are, so you can pursue partnerships and creative joint efforts with them. Don't be deceptive about it, just connect with them and see where it goes without any specific agenda.

By using influence-tracking tools (such as the ones I talk about on my resource page) in my own business I have been able to identify the most influential followers and customers of mine. Once I've identified who they are, it's easy for me to connect with them one-on-one and find out what they like and don't like about my business. They offer me great suggestions. I think every business could benefit greatly from making a special effort to connect with the most influential people in their circle of contacts.

# PART 19

# WE LIKE TO BUY FROM EXPERTS—SO BECOME AN EXPERT

*Conversations about you and your business are already happening online. You have three choices: You can ignore it, you can engage and join in, or you can become an expert and shape the conversation.*

I've probably convinced you by now that people want to do business with experts they know they can trust. How will you adjust your efforts accordingly?

When you imagine an expert, what comes to mind? Is it an old stuffy professor leaning on a chalkboard struggling to communicate deep and difficult concepts in simple enough terms that his young eager students can grasp? Maybe it's a clean-cut motivational speaker onstage with a $200 haircut and a smile to match delivering his latest amazing insights with a flowing style. If any of these images, or any elite feeling pops into your mind when I say expert, then you've become a bit out of touch with how the Internet works.

Whether we like it or not, the perception of who is and isn't an expert has now shifted dramatically thanks to search engines, online video, and the ease of distribution of all types of information around the world. You don't have to wait for a mega-news corporation or major publisher to come along and anoint you an expert any longer. The first step to becoming an expert is to call yourself one, and the second (a bit harder) step is to earn it every day by staying up-to-date on your content, and by creating and managing the conversations around your niche. Join forums where your expertise is needed and contribute in useful ways. Look for conversations on Twitter regarding your niche and help those that are discussing the topic. Experts are needed—it's time to step up.

How can you do all this?

You can't—not overnight, anyway. Baby steps will be taken for a few months and then, with focused effort, good fortune will suddenly start to reward your steady efforts (I've seen it happen repeatedly). Finally, you'll be the expert that everyone is seeking out. I did it myself in a *very* crowded niche market; I've helped hundreds of others do it, and you can do it to.

It all starts with a mindset change, though. You likely need to adjust your thoughts to include far less selling, pitching, and marketing. Start thinking more about engaging, leading, and authenticity.

# CHAPTER 88

# EXPERTS MAKE VIDEOS—SO MAKE VIDEOS

**I**n Part 10 I talked about making effective videos. This chapter is my attempt to convince you that you simply cannot ignore video and still be considered an expert. I want to show you how simple it can be.

You don't have to put your face or your voice in the videos; however your value as an expert will go way up if you can be brave enough to include yourself in the video. Spending some time surfing on YouTube, checking out what others in your niche market are doing, will help you determine what sort of effort you might make in the video arena.

Even starting out as simply as shooting short videos of you discussing relevant topics in two to three minute segments would be a fantastic start. There is no editing needed, and you don't have to look perfect. The more authentic you look and sound, the better received your video will probably be. In other words, just be yourself.

If you have the ability or the resources to clean up your videos a bit and improve the sound or lighting, of course your audience will appreciate the effort, but there is no public standard established for what you and your online videos must look or sound like before they are qualified to be considered expert content. The quality of the content is what really matters.

## EXPERTISE ESTABLISHED WITH SIMPLE VIDEO

My friend and colleague Mike LeMoine established a very successful Internet marketing consulting business in Albuquerque, New Mexico. His strategy for finding new clients simply involves creating video messages for the business owners that he is targeting for his services. The simplicity of these videos cannot be overstated. Mike simply talks into an inexpensive camera or webcam, and tells each business owner what he would like to do for them.

He lets them know as well that if they aren't interested, or if they don't reply, he will gladly take his services to a competitor because he can only work with one business in each niche in his area.

Since Mike now has a proven track record of being able to help businesses gain exposure, prospects, and new customers using creative Internet strategies, there is now no shortage of new clients who are interested in working with him. In less than two years his business, Maverick Web Video LLC, has grown from a one-man operation into a 10-person team that actively serves over 30 loyal clients as of this writing.

*About Mike LeMoine*: Mike started out as a newsletter reader of mine just a few short years ago, and now he's a valuable partner on multiple projects including the 9,000+ member membership site OfflineBiz.com where he's a VIP forum moderator and contributing expert.

# CHAPTER 89

# START A COACHING OR MENTORING PROGRAM

No matter what niche area your expertise happens to be in, I'm sure there's a way for you to benefit from offering coaching or mentoring services to your prospects and customers, or even to others that are in the same business you are in.

As you begin to succeed and mature in your business or leadership skills, you should look around and notice who else out there might benefit from your experiences and life skills. Survey these potential students and find out how you might best help them. Success is often something that successful people take for granted, but for every successful person there are hundreds or even thousands of others looking up to that person wondering how they do what they do. This eager audience needs your help and it could be profitable for you in the process. Even if you don't charge any money for your coaching or mentoring efforts, the additional credibility and influence that you will garner will make it more than worth the effort.

People from all over the world pay thousands of dollars each just to be able to join me and a couple of other experts on a series of conference calls where we teach and train specific strategies for marketing or Internet success. Why are people willing to pay such sums to be trained? My theory is that any of us can easily become stuck in a rut until we manage to free up either time or money to spare. If you have neither you can't advance, but if you have *either* then there is hope for you to improve yourself and advance your dreams. Coaching and mentoring with an expert is designed for those that lack time, but have the investment capital to pay true expert leaders to help them shorten the learning curve on any given life or business skill set. If all you have is time, then you'll have to take the slower path of learning on your own (until you have some money to invest in your business growth via a good mentor or coach).

Do all mentors charge money for their services? Of course not, but what would you do if a steady stream of 30 new people every day were asking for your advice and coaching on a process that could put thousands of dollars per month or more into their pockets? That's the fortunate situation I've found myself in, so I now offer (on a limited basis) paid coaching for those seeking my help. It's something every expert should consider because even if you only have a few clients per year, you'll be perceived as an expert and an ever-increasing stream of new clients will come your way as a result. We've established that people like buying from knowledgeable experts—so become one!

I published a popular article a few years ago on my blog and it rings just as true now as it ever did. Maybe it will help you see yourself as an in-demand expert. Here's a summary of the concept.

## THE TWO STEPS TO MASSIVE SUCCESS IN THE INFORMATION AGE

So what are the two steps to success that are used by so many others including me?

STEP ONE: Make a success story out of yourself. It doesn't have to be a huge success story, but enough so that you are proud of where you find yourself. You can make mistakes along the way—just document them.

STEP TWO: Profit as you teach others how you did it. Plenty of people haven't even started yet, and your free advice and training will be invaluable to them. They are waiting for you to show up.

Not very profound, is it?

If someone had told me that exact information when I was starting out, it would have inspired me to move more quickly towards my goals.

# CHAPTER 90

# TEACHING IS FREE MARKETING

**W**hat do libraries, community centers, small business associations, meetup.com groups, chambers of commerce groups, and community colleges all have in common?

They all need teachers and presenters.

Once you've established a bit of credibility and expertise in any niche market, you can easily approach organizations and volunteer your services to help educate other business owners or even other general audiences on topics of interest to them. Even if you don't make any sales it is still a very worthwhile experience for you to get in front of a group and present your ideas, your successes, and your failures. True leaders are always good teachers, so every chance you have to improve your teaching skills you should accept. This is how you'll build your reputation and skills as an expert presenter in your niche market. Be sure to have someone take plenty of pictures too!

---

## EXAMPLE

At OfflineBiz.com we teach Internet enthusiasts how to apply basic marketing skills to real-world businesses and get paid handsomely for it. This is a much-needed service among businesses that are floundering online, and the skills we teach our "consultants in training" are quickly learned through the courses and content that we provide on the site.

*(continued)*

---

(*Continued*)

Once the members of OfflineBiz.com feel adequately trained and ready to start approaching businesses, we offer them a few suggestions on how to find their first clients. Among other ideas, one of the *ideal* (and bravest) courses of action is for them to **arrange speaking engagements in front of small groups of business owners** so that they can present some basic ideas for success on the Internet. Inevitably these types of engagements lead to great things.

Giving away fantastic content and free information that fellow business owners can immediately apply is a great way to establish expertise in the minds of potential prospects.

If you've had any level of success at all in business, then you have an eager audience waiting to learn from you exactly how you did it. Budding entrepreneurs worldwide eagerly devour the advice and attention of those who have already accomplished what they hope to accomplish someday. That could easily be your next audience.

Occasionally I'll visit Twitter.com and post a simple message that says something like, "How can I help your business today?" The resulting conversations always lead to some type of positive interaction and great exposure for my services as well as the businesses that I assist. Maintain this type of synergy and exposure by keeping a teacher's mentality in every aspect of your business efforts.

# CHAPTER 91

# CREATING AUDIOS AND PODCASTING

\

*A podcast is a series of digital media files (either audio or video) that are*
*released episodically and often downloaded through web syndication.*
—Wikipedia Definition of Podcasting

For this chapter I only refer to audio recordings (your voice) when addressing podcasting. The vast majority of podcasters are creating audio files as opposed to video.

I've not done a lot of podcasting myself, but I have created hundreds of short audios as content for my audience. Frequently I'll add these audios to my blog, or include a link in my newsletter so that my readers can easily listen in if they are interested.

There is plenty of help online if you get stuck at any point in the process.

Recording yourself and posting that audio online is a very simple way to put a lot of power behind your message. The potential for your audio message to be spread virally is significant, and the expense of posting the audio online is nominal.

I love creating audio because of how quickly I can get the content out of my head and into a stored format. Oftentimes the idea of writing down the details of an idea that I have can zap the energy out of the idea. With audio that's not the case. It's just a matter of talking into a microphone.

**Getting set up:**
- You will need a decent headset with a microphone. I use a $50 Log-itech headset that covers both ears and has the microphone that extends forward. There is no need to spend any more than $50 or so on your

headset especially when you are just getting started with audio recording. There are several options for capturing audio on your computer including online services, but I suggest you start with the free software, Audacity. More on that below.

- Don't script out everything that you will be saying. I typically use a small note card with three to five bullet points that I want to be sure and address. If you're familiar with your subject matter, just begin discussing it. At the beginning of your recording be sure to tell your listeners who you are, and what you'll be talking about. I've found that shorter audios are more likely to be listened to than are longer ones. Imagine yourself talking to one person when recording. Don't address your listeners as a group no matter how large your audience is. This will help you connect in an authentic way.

- Try to record your audios while standing up. Also smile and pay attention to your posture. As strange as it may sound, your body language is conveyed through the microphone even when you are simply recording an audio (this is a great telephone skill as well). Your audience will never be more interested in a subject than you are. You don't have to use a "radio voice" to be effective. Be authentic, just be you, but be interested in the subject you're talking about. Keep your microphone adjusted so that it is slightly above or below your mouth. This will help prevent a popping sound when you use the letter $p$.

- To do basic editing on your audio I suggest you start out with the free software called Audacity, which is available at the website audacity.sourceforge.net. Audacity software makes it easy to add in intro and exit music, as well as perform basic editing on your audio. Under the Preferences tab in Audacity you will find a setting to adjust the bit rate of your recording. The bit rate for voice recordings should be 64 kbps. There's no need to go higher in most cases.

- There are several sources of royalty-free music that can be used as an introduction for your recording. A quick search on Google for the phrase "royalty free music" should produce several options. Audacity can be used to insert these optional features.

- Often times I'll simply use my WordPress blog file upload feature to store my audios right on my blog. Since I have an e-mail list of subscribers, I'll make them aware of my audios as new blog posts and they can listen in on their schedule.

- If you want to take it a step farther, you can post the MP3 file to iTunes or other podcast directories (do a Google search for "podcast directories"). Using a tool like PowerPress from blubrry.com as a plug-in on your WordPress blog allows you to automate the process of adding new audio blog posts as content that is also sent directly to iTunes and other directories. You can access plug-ins directly from the control panel of your blog—it takes about 15 seconds to add them onto your blog in most cases. Dedicate a category on your blog to your podcast episodes, and then use the PowerPress category-specific RSS feed so that only your podcast episodes are sent to iTunes and other directories (you don't want to send your written posts to the podcast directories). Once you have the plug-in installed on your blog site there will be a new input field on your "make a new blog post" page. Enter your show notes as if you were typing a new blog post, and then enter the link that points to your MP3 file. You'll have a nice play button inserted into your blog post and you'll be creating podcasts simultaneously.

- If you start distributing your audios to iTunes and other podcast sites, you'll want to pay attention to your ID3 tags. This is where information such as your episode title, artist or band name, any artwork associated with the file, and so on is stored. There are several ID3 tag editors on the market. Check out the ID3 Editor (available from pa-software.com) for one option. The keywords you use in these tags will help potential listeners find you, and will add a professional touch to your podcast.

I am unaware of the exact statistics, but I can tell you that podcasting is not a path to overnight fame online. Creating audios and sharing them with your audience is a fantastic way to build rapport and to connect with an audience that you already have. It is also a good way to find a steady stream of new fans and followers because of all of the traffic and listeners hanging out on iTunes, but the overnight success stories just aren't there. As with any other marketing effort, be sure to track your results, and adjust your strategy if necessary.

Check out some of the popular podcasts offered on iTunes and see if you can spot trends in how they market themselves and connect with their audiences. The rules are far different than traditional radio broadcasting. If I had to identify one common denominator among all of the most successful podcasters, it would be their ability to connect and be authentic with their audience.

# CHAPTER 92

# USE LEVERAGE TO GROW YOUR BRAND FAST

**L**everage is a simple concept to me. By choosing the right tool for the job you can apply the smallest amount of effort in the shortest amount of time and get the greatest possible results.

Understanding and applying the concept of leverage is more important now than perhaps at any point in business history. I make this statement for several reasons, including the fact that change is occurring more rapidly than at any other point, and innumerable new tools are being introduced continually. If you don't remain a student of leverage, you can be left behind quickly.

To illustrate my point with a construction analogy, imagine if the tools of home construction were changing as rapidly as are the tools of social media connection, information sharing, and content distribution. In my illustration, hardware stores would be completely changing their entire inventory of tools and replacing them with better, faster, and cheaper tools almost monthly. New stores would be opening and closing rapidly. What worked last year would stop working suddenly and homebuilders would become increasingly reliant on trusted advisers to help them navigate their options. The homebuilders that chose to ignore these trends would find it nearly impossible to produce a competitive product as a result. I'm sure those in the housing industry would agree that some version of what I've just said is already true, but by choosing to participate in the information economy you will be in the heart of the storm.

Being a student of leverage and dedicating some time every week to reading material by thought leaders is essential if you are to keep up. That's why I always teach business owners to work *on* their businesses, not *in* them.

I introduced several tools in this book that can be leveraged to your benefit, but more important than any given tool or strategy is a mindset that is continually open to the leverage opportunities that are all around you.

## LEVERAGE YOU

No one has the same circle of influence, friends, or experiences that you do. All of these connections and lessons are entities that can be leveraged. Even your story can be leveraged.

One word of caution: While leverage certainly can be applied to relationships, you should never consider any sort of arrangement that does not include a huge win for all parties involved. If you can master the art of leveraging your relationships while keeping the best interests of the other party fully in focus, you will have learned a powerful business and marketing skill.

It amazes me how willing people are sometimes to throw out everything they've learned, and the experiences that they've had, in order to pursue a completely new line of opportunity that they know very little about. I often refer to this as shiny-object chasing. Sadly, many entrepreneurs fall prey to this nasty habit and as a result they find themselves with a long track record of attempted and failed business ventures. Even harsh lessons can be leveraged into a fantastic opportunity however. History is full of examples of great accomplishments that finally came after years of false starts.

Make a list of all of the available resources, tools, relationships, and experiences that you could leverage. If you can't come up with at least 100 items to leverage for your list, then you haven't been paying attention.

# CHAPTER 93

# TELESEMINARS ARE INSTANT EXPERT CONTENT

Experts are always educating. Experts are always creating content. One of the most reliable tools that you can use to capture a steady stream of fantastic content is the good old telephone.

Teleseminars are one of my favorite ways to capture amazing content and to communicate with an audience, either live or with the recording of a call. A teleseminar is nothing more than a recorded telephone conversation among two or more people. As soon as the call is over you have an MP3 recording that can be edited or used as is. It can be transcribed and turned into a book if you so desire. It's instant, easy content.

Typically the teleseminar is a presentation conducted by one, or at most three or four, hosts, while a large number of audience participants can listen in and, in some cases, interact with the hosts. The only thing that distinguishes a host from a participant is control of the recording and mute features of the call.

The only thing you need is a free account with freeconferencecall.com, skype.com, or any other similar service. You could host a teleseminar five minutes from now if you wanted to. They don't have to be scheduled—all you need is two or more people on the phone and then press the record button.

On many occasions I've arranged to interview or discuss interesting topics with an expert in my industry by way of a simple teleseminar call. Sometimes I'll invite a live audience to listen in as well by sharing a specific date and time with my audience so they can join in and listen.

If I have a live audience I can mute and unmute them as the host for a question-and-answer session while recording the entire event. With more than a handful of people on the line at a time, the background noise can easily get out of hand, so the primary host needs to be ready to mute all participants whenever necessary. Individual participants can also mute themselves, so only those with questions can be heard and recorded. With more than 10 people or so on the line, the odds of background noise go up dramatically unless you have control of the mute features of the service you are using.

I've conducted training courses where students paid thousands of dollars to receive the training and coaching I delivered, and the entire content of the course consisted of recorded teleseminar sessions that were later transcribed into printable documents.

### Some tips from a teleseminar veteran:

- Always start out the call by introducing yourself briefly and then the expert/guest thoroughly. Give any guest expert recognition for whatever accomplishments or websites they told you (prior to the call) that they would like to have mentioned. Halfway through and at the end of the call remind your listeners who they've been listening to, and also remind them, briefly, again of the book or website that your expert is pitching.
- At the start of the call briefly summarize the topics that you'll be covering in the order that you'll be covering them. Your listeners will appreciate that they can fast forward to the points most interesting to them.
- Keep the energy level up by being excited about the topic and content. Your audience won't be more into it than you are.
- Try not to breathe into the headset and remind your other hosts of the same rule. Make sure your other hosts make liberal use of the mute feature. If a barking dog or other interruption enters the scene on a host, it is their job to mute it.
- If any of the hosts seem to have a bad connection, have them immediately hang up and dial back in. Use a land line whenever possible, never a cell phone unless entirely unavoidable. Don't stick too closely to a script. Let the call flow freely.
- Two or more hosts are better than one. Each host should say something every few minutes. Don't let one person ramble on too long or it gets boring.
- Give participants a warning when you are about to ask questions so that they are ready for it—otherwise you'll have dead air when you flip the mute switch and invite them to join in. All hosts give each other permission to gently interrupt and occasionally talk over each other so that it sounds less scripted and more like a real conversation

(picture the news commentary shows with guests—don't worry about being polite). This type of banter is easy to listen to, but polite pauses between each speaker will make the audio seem to drag on.

- Make sure that you share these tips with the other call hosts well ahead of time. Shorter calls that leave your audience wanting more are always better than longer calls that end awkwardly and slowly. Tell everyone how to get more help if they need it.
- At more than one place in the call announce who you are, who you are interviewing, and what the content of the call is. Educate, don't pitch. Consider having a silent assistant join you on the line as a host so they can control the mute/unmute features of the participants, as well as the recording start and stop feature. On a large call with many participants it's nice to have someone greet people as they show up on the call (unmuted) and ask their names and where they are from, as well as introduce the main hosts when you are ready to begin. Another responsibility that this silent assistant can perform is to monitor an e-mail account where questions can be submitted in real time for the presenters to answer as they come in. The assistant can pass the good questions to the presenters, and answer the less broadcast-worthy questions individually. Don't let the call go longer than 45 minutes to an hour. Schedule a second call if necessary.
- Provide the expert with a handful of questions before the interview begins and allow the expert to add in their own questions as well. Don't spend too much time scripting the interview though—instead let it flow naturally as a conversation. For added value, create a list of time marks and topics covered in the audio and add that information near the download link for your interview. This makes the audio far more usable when posted on your blog or other website. See the chapter on podcasting for ideas on posting and sharing audio content.

## IMPROMPTU RECORDINGS

Have you ever been on the phone with someone and had such an interesting conversation that the two of you wished you had recorded the whole thing? Don't let this happen to you. You can sign up for a free account with any number of free conference call services in a matter of seconds.

Frequently when I have the opportunity to connect on the phone with someone interesting or passionate about any subject, I will ask them to dial into my freeconferencecall.com phone number so that we can easily record the conversation for future use. This is just one more creative way to capture quick content. A great example of this is found at the end of Chapter 30 where I had an excited student of mine request to talk to me. I e-mailed him back and asked his permission to record the call and he agreed. I sent him my conference dial-in info and I'm so glad I did. You can listen to the results for yourself if you'd like. I do this type of thing all the time and it costs me nothing to capture this amazing content.

## CHAPTER 94

# WEBINARS AS THE ULTIMATE CUSTOMER FOLLOW-UP AND PRESENTATION TOOL

**W**ebinars are used by many marketers as an effective education and communication tool. The term *webinar* comes from squishing the words web (as in Internet) and seminar together.

These online seminars typically include a PowerPoint-type slide presentation delivered with a small number of presenters discussing the content to any number of participants that have dialed in on a traditional phone, or they are listening over their Internet connection.

A typical webinar is either a live event viewed online by participants, or it's a recorded presentation that is stored online for easy viewing later.

Participating in a webinar online has many of the same benefits of attending a live presentation. Depending on what service you use to conduct your webinar, you can even take live questions or interact with the other attendees. Live video feed webinars are now possible as well, and in all cases these online events can be recorded and played back later for those that can't attend.

Some of the most powerful webinars that I've been a part of were conducted by qualified experts who moved at a good pace through a PowerPoint-style slide show and took questions from the audience regarding content. Effective webinars should never be positioned as a sales pitch. They should be informative, engaging, and contain useful information. Any selling should be done via a very soft sell at the end of the presentation.

The same skills that you'd use when presenting a PowerPoint-style slide show come into play when presenting in a webinar.

- Use your slides to enhance what the speaker is saying, never read from the slides.
- Have a printout of all your slides nearby so that you can easily jump or skip slides if necessary.
- No one is impressed by cheesy scrolling graphics. Don't use them.
- Fewer slides are always better than more slides. Presenting a webinar runs a great risk for you becoming irrelevant or boring since it's difficult to see the expressions of your listeners.

The most common live webinar services that I am aware of are: GoToWebinar.com, Webex.com, Adobe Acrobat Connect Pro, Microsoft's Office Live Meeting, and Verizon Web Conferencing. I have successfully used prerecorded webinars and then have them run on a set schedule with ongoing promotions for each occurrence. More on that topic follows in the Power Tools section of this chapter.

Typically, for live presentations, the presenter or presenters have the option to present from either a video camera (webcam) or by audio only using VOIP or a standard phone line. All services allow you to turn on the sharing of your screen for the presentation so those attending can see what you see.

**Some observations from the best webinars I've been a part of:**
- If you are trying to sell something at the conclusion of the webinar, have a phone number that people can call to talk to someone live before they make a decision. This will greatly increase your conversion rate. If the main speaker is on hand to conduct some of the live Q/A you will do even better.
- The more interactive the webinar is, the more likely your viewers are to feel engaged. This is always a good thing.
- If a large audience is in attendance it is a good idea to show the number of attendees on the screen in some fashion. Allowing them to chat live and see each other's questions isn't always a good idea depending on the audience. All it takes is one troublemaker to throw a bad twist on the whole event. Be prepared to cut off anyone that is obviously just making trouble. Be familiar with the controls and have someone besides the presenter as a wingman to manage such incidents.
- Most webinar services will have the ability for you to mute and unmute your guests either individually or as a group. Take advantage of this feature to field questions from the audience at appropriate times.

- Inevitably some people that attend your sales webinar will fall into the "Maybe" category. These are the people that aren't saying "Yes" to your offer nor are they saying "No." Be prepared to offer them some sort of follow-up alternative that helps them become more comfortable with the content and the product being offered. You can make many sales in the days and weeks following a good webinar by following up with your "Maybe" leads.
- If you intend to record a webinar and use the content on an ongoing or recurring basis, you should be careful not to mention specific dates or events that would make the content seem to be out of date for future viewers. Even if all of the content is 100 percent current and relevant, a presenter accidentally mentioning the two teams playing in a major sporting event will give the audience a clue about the date of the recording. Once your material is dated the audience could lose interest before they give your content consideration.

I've effectively combined the power of automated e-mail marketing with the power of webinars. Whenever I've participated in a powerful webinar, I capture the content and permanently store it online where it can be viewed at any time. I then add a follow-up message to the appropriate e-mail campaigns so all future subscribers can be exposed to the great content. I make it clear that the event was previously recorded, because it could be viewed at 3 A.M. if the prospect chooses to watch it then.

A powerful strategy for webinars is to schedule them to run at repeating, set intervals so you can promote the material as if it were "live" to new sets of prospects on an ongoing basis. This works well as long as the content is fresh, and you are prepared for the questions or phone calls that come in inevitably each time it runs. That's where great webinar and follow-up power tools come in.

## WEBINAR POWER TOOLS

I'm using a tool called "Instant Customer" for my webinar needs because of the insanely high level of follow up and customization that it allows.

While you can't do a live event with "Instant Customer" (yet), this isn't really a restriction. You can get your prerecorded webinar presentation perfect beforehand, and then replay it over and over again as if it were live by running it on a set schedule. The promotional website and all related messages automatically adjust for each new run. Just be prepared to take questions by phone or e-mail each time the event is played. This means scheduling it for a time when someone is there to help those that might have questions.

By having a pre-webinar sign-up page hosted by the Instant Customer service, you can engage with your prospects in previously unimaginable ways.

For example, you can automatically connect after the webinar with everyone that didn't show up and tell them that you missed seeing them and then also give them a link to the recording.

You can even customize the follow-up messages that go out automatically to those that decide to leave early, or those that come in late for the scheduled event!

You can send out a text message reminder that tells prospects that the webinar they signed up for is about to start.

Better yet, you can send an automated text message that pings everyone that leaves early telling them that you noticed they had to drop out, and gives them a call-in number if they have any questions along with a copy of the replay link.

You can also identify who the most influential participants will be and contact them proactively before or after the call. For example, the first time I used the service I easily identified the most influential participants who had signed up and sent them this message: "Thanks for signing up for our webinar about XYZ. This is Jim and I'll be the live presenter. I noticed that you are among one of the most socially influential people that signed up for our webinar. Would you mind if I touch base with you personally? I have a lot of respect for the great level of social influence you've achieved online and I love connecting with the "big hitters" in our industry."

You can also send the recorded presentation to everyone that signed up, but didn't show up.

That's putting follow up and customer contact on the cutting edge. These types of tools are here now. Learn to use them!

On my resource page I have more information about the Instant Customer tool and how I've used it very successfully. With emerging tools like this you can engage with an audience no matter how large it is, on a never-before-seen personal level.

# CHAPTER 95

# IMPROVE ON WHAT WORKED BEFORE

This may seem strange to point out, but on multiple occasions I've had an "aha moment" with clients when I asked them one simple question.

That simple question is this: What did you do last year that worked best? Or, what was the best marketing idea you ever used to help grow your business?

Better yet, what are you doing to sell more things to your most loyal customers?

As entrepreneurs I think we have a tendency to be so forward-looking that we forget to look back and review what we've done that did and didn't work. If you don't have an established location where you store records of the ideas that have and haven't worked for you, then odds are you aren't addressing this issue properly. I like to use a tool called *evernote* from EverNote.com for this purpose. It's a free downloadable app that you should look into.

Spend some time thinking back on the last few years of your business and try to recall the promotions or ideas that worked best. Revisit those ideas and see if there are any ways that you could automate or expand on them in order to make them better than ever.

An active member of OfflineBiz.com, and a respected colleague of mine, Hanif Khaki* does a lot of marketing consulting with various businesses. He recently sent me a couple of stories that are a perfect example of what I'm talking about.

In the first example, Hanif was able to get over 10 percent of an insurance broker's current clients to sign up for a new e-mail list and get engaged using one simple letter and a simple, one-page website to collect the names and e-mail addresses.

The client needed a way to engage current clients and also wanted a way to communicate with them more cost effectively, and an e-mail list was a perfect fit, but he didn't have one yet.

Solution: They sent out a "Thank you/Invitation" letter as a ride-along with a calendar that was being mailed during the holiday season. Since this was an annual mailing that was set to occur anyway, no additional mailing costs were incurred. This single letter resulted in cultivating very good will, new forms of client engagement, and a 10 percent-plus conversion rate of clients going online as a result of an incentive and opting into an e-mail list. This has lead to numerous new sales with virtually no marketing expenses incurred.

In the second example, Hanif was working with a heating and cooling company.

The challenge was this: While his client knew that many of his current customers had aging HVAC systems, he also knew that they weren't likely to call him until their systems broke down. Hanif convinced him that it would be a great service to his clients if they were made aware of the benefits of upgrading *before* it became more expensive and absolutely necessary.

Together, they segmented those customers who were the most likely to benefit from in-home HVAC-system checkups and sent them all a letter from the President encouraging them to request a free inspection appointment. For every 100 letters mailed, 10 responded and set-up appointments. Two out of each 10 appointments resulted in a high-margin sale. All who made appointments also had their contact info captured on an online database for easy future follow up.

*Hanif Khaki is President of Phase 3 Marketing Inc.

# CHAPTER 96

# EMBRACE OUTSOURCING FOR SOME OF YOUR MARKETING EFFORTS

**I**f you find yourself working *in* your business more than you are working *on* your business, then something is out of order and you won't grow as quickly or as large as you should be.

Any repetitive or technically challenging projects that you find yourself trying to tackle on your own should be passed off to someone else that can do the job more easily, faster, and, in most cases, better than you could ever do it yourself. Your time is the premium asset that you should be protecting when it comes to making business decisions. The more time you can free up, and the less money you can spend freeing it up, the more successful you'll become, and the faster your business will grow.

Outsourcing (using sites like odesk.com, vworker.com, and elance.com) and crowdsourcing (using sites like 99designs.com and mturk.com) are becoming vital components of many successful businesses online and offline. Regardless of where you stand on the idea of using help from other countries outside of your own, the fact is that there are many skilled programmers, writers, web designers, and hosts of other talented people all over the planet. When I have a task to complete for my business, I don't limit my talent pool to only those that live inside of my own country. I open the job up to all eligible candidates.

## CROWDSOURCING DEFINED ON WIKIPEDIA

Crowdsourcing is a neologistic compound of Crowd and Outsourcing for the act of taking tasks traditionally performed by an employee or

286

contractor, and outsourcing them to a group of people or community, through an "open call" to a large group of people (a crowd) asking for contributions.

Few business owners realize it, but you can hire amazingly hard working, talented, honest, reliable help for a few dollars per hour in the Philippines. Filipinos love the U.S. dollar (and the Euro) because the currency goes so far in their country.

A family of four that has a head of household making just a few dollars per hour can live quite well by local standards, and steady jobs are very hard to find there currently.

In the Philippines there is an overabundance of talented, English speaking, skilled, tech-savvy workers ready and willing to go to work *today* to make your Internet business grow even while you sleep. I've hired web designers, writers, e-mail customer service agents, and content distribution experts from the Philippines.

The Filipino culture is characterized as hard working, honest, and not resentful of foreign employers, as some people might suspect they would. They are grateful for the work in most cases. Typically they love the chance to do meaningful work and they will thank you frequently for the chance to prove they are worthy of your trust.

John Jonas is my "go to" expert on all things related to outsourcing. He's given me several pointers over the years and we recorded a good audio lately on the subject covering everything you need to know about hiring someone from the Philippines. There is a free audio training on the resource page that will step you through the process of finding and hiring the best help possible for those tasks that can be outsourced. In the interest of full disclosure, there is a program the John sells for those that want his help, but the interview is very thorough, and you don't have to pay someone to help you find and hire a great worker from the Philippines.

I see many business owners become bogged down in doing the day-to-day tasks that could and should be passed off to someone else's capable hands. Think through the tasks that you perform yourself on a day-to-day basis. Are any of those tasks ones that could be passed to someone else if they were willing to work remotely for a few dollars per hour? If so, you should be focused on transitioning those responsibilities to someone else.

In my own business I am constantly evaluating the way I spend my time, and I've given away several of the mundane tasks that can easily clutter my day. I have a handful of part-time helpers locally who help me run my business, as well as workers in other nations doing Internet-based work for me. I think of all of it as outsourcing. Once I established the value of a business hour of my time, it was easy to justify investing some money to free up my time.

What work should you, as the owner, be doing? Focus in on working *on* your business instead of *in* your business. Think, create, plan, and do only the stuff you love to do. Try to leave the rest to others. Even if you love the work you are doing, be sure that you are dedicating significant time to replacing yourself. If you are unable to remove yourself from the equation of the day-to-day responsibilities of your business, you will never be able to take a break without losing income and you'll lose the ability to focus on expanding your business to the next level. There is also the factor of making your business transportable so that a new owner could buy and take over the business if it ever became necessary or desirable.

If you are trapped in the mentality of thinking that you are the best person to tackle every aspect of your business, then your business will never be very large, and it will own you as it grows. Do not allow your business to own you. Outsource the tasks that could and should be getting done by someone else.

## CHAPTER 97

# REPLACE ROI WITH RLC FOR BETTER MARKETING MONITORING

"**S**o Jim, what sort of *return on investment* (ROI) can I expect from using your ideas?"

Fair question.

Even though most of the ideas presented in this book have been free marketing ideas, you should still track the amount of time and even the small monetary investments that you make in implementing these ideas. You will almost certainly find, as so many others have, that 80 percent of your results come from 20 percent of your efforts, but you'll have to give it time.

Relationships take time.

We've heard the old saying, "I know that half of my advertising is working, but I just don't know which half." It has always been difficult to track the results of marketing and advertising efforts, and even though the Internet makes it a lot easier to track these things in *some* cases (such as when using pay-per-click marketing), it is still difficult to measure the full impact of most marketing efforts that you undertake. This is especially true once you begin to understand the power of building relationships using the Internet. It can be nearly impossible to track (from an ROI perspective) how well it's going. Your bottom line will certainly reflect it, but it might be a bit difficult to trace your results back to their source.

In this book I attempt to convince you that the best ideas for spreading your brand and increasing your customer base are more about *relationships and trust* than they are about spending money on the correct advertising or marketing systems. The best ideas are free ideas. Remember, I said in the introduction that marketing has been freed by the Internet.

How does this work in real life?

In Malcolm Gladwell's book *The Tipping Point* he lays out a new way of understanding why change, both positive and negative, happens so rapidly in some cases. Malcolm is trying to teach us how to start positive epidemics around our businesses or ideas.

I say there is another goal that is bigger than ROI and I call it the RLC metric. RLC should be your focus in order to create an unstoppable tipping point of positive activity about you and your brand.

Here's how my theory of RLC works:

Create your own positive tipping point by staying focused on *Relationships, Leadership, and Creativity* (RLC) instead of on ROI.

When analyzing a new marketing or advertising effort, attempt to measure the likely impact on your RLC score. If an event, activity, website, product, advertisement, or even new employee doesn't fit into your RLC goals, then why are you doing it? Customers are observing and talking about every aspect of your business online even if you haven't joined in the conversation yet. What are you giving them to talk about?

You'll know you've reached a tipping point when the crowd is doing much of your work for you. At that point the ROI becomes entirely irrelevant and impossible to track, but the results are undeniable.

If you are a die-hard fan of tracking the ROI of your marketing and advertising efforts then I have a few questions for you.

- What is the ROI of creating a new, raving fan that has just seen your YouTube video that addresses his most pressing questions? You posted the video three years ago—how can you track that?
- What is the ROI of having a raving fan with a popular blog excitedly describing his take on your latest product without even asking your permission to write the article?
- What is the ROI of your special report being passed virally around the Internet in virtually untraceable ways and adding dozens of new fans to your e-mail list daily as a result?
- What is the ROI of a customer bragging to 2,500 Facebook friends about the amazing service and meal he just had at your restaurant?
- What's the ROI of offering your services for free to the 25 most socially influential people in your area (i.e. highest klout.com score) in the hopes that they will share the ideas with others in their social circle?

- What is the ROI of getting invited to speak in front of a large targeted audience at a large conference because of your established reputation as an industry expert?

For example, in my own business I can rely on a steady stream of new e-mail subscribers and customers flowing into my business every day without me having to do any new marketing or advertising. When I do work, I am focusing on one of three things: Relationships, Leadership, and Creativity. These have been the core principles of my business for a long time now, and I can assure you that the ROI for my efforts is off the charts, although I have no idea how to begin to track it (nor do I care to).

**You Focus On:**
- Relationships: Genuine interest in the welfare of those you work with and for.
- Leadership: Be an expert. Act like an expert. Share your expertise openly. Make trends—don't follow them.
- Creativity: Be the first to try new things that haven't been done. It might feel irrational, but if it's shareable it could spread like mad.

If you do these things well, you'll hit a tipping point and you'll be rewarded with:

- Influence that expands exponentially.
- Trust you barely have to work for.
- A self-perpetuating, positive reputation.

Once you hit this tipping point, the odds are stacked in your favor. The conversations, testimonials, firsthand accounts, and fans online will all have your back, and all you have to do is continue to nurture and protect your RLC. Do the same things that got you to that point.

## A WARNING

It is impossible to please everyone, nor should you try to. If you try to, you'll actually have a greater number of unhappy customers. Don't worry about those that aren't in your target audience. Find creative ways to fire the customers that just don't get it.

To borrow a customer service phrase from Seth Godin's blog: "Pleasing everyone with our work is impossible. It wastes the time of our best customers and annoys our staff. Forgive us for focusing on those we're trying to delight."

## Speed Up the Process with Leverage

Want to speed up the whole process? Apply leverage. Part six of this book, as well as Chapters 67 and 92, address applying leverage. You can drastically speed up the results you'll get while focusing on Relationships, Leadership, and Creativity if you apply leverage to the process.

A final point: The greatest tool for business leverage ever known to humankind is the Internet.

# CHAPTER 98

# PLAY MARKETING OFFENSE WITH GOOGLE ALERTS

E arlier in the book I talk about defending your reputation by using Google Alerts. As a reminder, Google Alerts is a free tool that automatically e-mails you any time the keywords that you specify are used anywhere online.

Here are several ways to proactively use Google Alerts as a weapon of "offense."

- If you are trying to establish a connection with an influential person in your industry, try using Google Alerts to follow that person's name. When you see their name pop up in an article or on a discussion forum, join in or contribute to the comments in a creative or useful way.
- If you are aware of any topics that your target influencer is interested in, use Google Alerts to follow those keywords and then when you see an article that you think may be of interest to them, send them a link to it along with a note. If you can drop a printed article in the mail, that will carry even more significance.
- Follow the industry trends and stories related to your niche and write blog posts responding to them. Take strong stands on controversial subjects so you establish your credibility as a leader in your field. Even those people that disagree with you will respect the fact that you stand up for the principles that you believe in.
- Set up Google Alerts for all of the employees, partners, and top customers that your business serves. Any time something of note happens online with one of these parties send them a quick note recognizing the accomplishment.

- One of the best ways to get fantastic new marketing ideas is to follow the online marketing activities of either your competitors, or of other businesses that cater to your same demographic. By using Google Alerts to locate and follow similar businesses around the world you can observe those businesses and learn a great deal about what does and doesn't seem to be working for them. As you find creative businesses to follow, also consider joining their mailing lists to catch the content that Google misses.

# PART 20

# GRAB BAG OF IDEAS

In this final part of the book are several ideas that didn't fit neatly in other places.

This is also a great time to remind you that you can find several more ideas listed on the resource page for this book at 101FreeMarketing.com.

As more people read the book, there will be even more ideas posted on that page, so I'm hoping that page becomes a good resource for you with several new creative ideas for growing your business using free or nearly free marketing strategies.

## CHAPTER 99

# COLLABORATION ISN'T COMPLICATED ANYMORE

In the late 1990s I was a sales rep for a channel partner of Microsoft. I remember when the most exciting new word in business was collaboration. Back then it was a marvel to think that people from all over the world could work together simultaneously on the same spreadsheet posted online.

## SIDE NOTE

I've gone from relying almost exclusively on Microsoft products as a former diehard channel sales rep for Microsoft, to relying almost exclusively on free products such as OpenOffice.org and Gmail.com which have virtually replaced my need for any paid software products in the email, document, spreadsheet, presentation arena. I've never encountered a compatibility issue either. Everything is very cross-compatible now. This book was composed as an OpenOffice text document and sent to the publisher as a Microsoft-compatible document.

Most businesses in the mid-1990s didn't quite grasp the idea of online collaboration, and to this day most businesses still don't use it to its fullest potential.

I don't think that the concept of collaboration really took off for most small businesses until it became virtually free to engage in online.

Using the tools of collaboration that are freely available online, I've built huge businesses that are being managed and influenced by people from all over the planet. Embracing a philosophy of collaboration is key if you are to achieve your full potential online.

Odds are, you are already using collaboration in one form or another without even realizing it.

Here are some simple examples of collaboration that you're likely familiar with, along with some free tools that you may not know exist, but some of which should be added to your marketing and business arsenal.

- Post a new idea on Facebook and ask your followers what they think of it is a form of creative collaboration. I did that with this book!
- This book includes a resource page where I invite my readers to openly discuss and comment about the content of this book (101FreeMarketing.com). I don't pretend to be the world's foremost expert on all possible marketing topics. I rely on collaboration with my readers so that the truly amazing ideas can flow to the top for all of us. That's collaboration.
- Use a free Google calendar application that can openly be edited by those you invite as contributors, and then openly viewed for all prospects to see. This is great for organizations such as churches or other groups with a central leadership that has various event tracking needs.
- Use the documents feature of Gmail (called *Google Docs*) to put together presentations, spreadsheets, or any other kind of document as a team. Anyone that is invited to contribute can edit and/or see the document in progress.
- Use Twitter as a real-time collaboration tool with a group of any size. Hash tags (#) make it easy for all of you to monitor all posts related to the topic you wish to follow.
- Enable blog comments on your blog and install a plug-in that allows readers to respond to the comments left by others. Pay attention to what gets the most attention. Let them help solve each other's problems.
- When you post videos to YouTube, encourage and invite comments and ideas from those that view the video. Ask them what else they'd like to see. Let them collaborate on your future efforts.

## FREE AND INEXPENSIVE TOOLS FOR COLLABORATION

Dropbox.com: File storage and sharing. Hard Return Google Docs: Document creation and sharing.

Freeconferencecall.com: Free conference call and recording service.

Jott.com: Turn voice and memo into an e-mail.

# CHAPTER 100

# SPLIT TEST FOR MARKETING POWER

**I**f I had to name the one activity that separates the big dogs from the rest of the crowd in the marketing industry it would be split testing.

**Split testing is achieved with the following steps:**
- Establish a baseline response rate to an offer or call to action.
- Create a second call to action or offer with one feature slightly adjusted (typically the headline).
- Send most of your traffic to the established baseline offer.
- Send a portion of your traffic to the second call to action until you have a large enough sample size to determine (with statistically significant certainty) if the second offer is outperforming the first or not.
- Once the second offer is determined not to be outperforming the first offer, it is scrapped and replaced with a new offer until a new winning offer establishes a new baseline response rate.

There are websites, blogs, and books dedicated to teaching the power of split testing and marketing. The good news is you can easily take advantage of the power of split testing by using some basic free tools.

Even if you don't want to dive deeply into the world of split testing every aspect of your marketing message, it could still really pay off to split test some of the most influential parts of your marketing message.

# CHAPTER 101

# COOL MARKETING
# BRAIN FOOD

$T$aking a few minutes to explore the marketing ideas behind these sites is time well spent:

Fiverr.com: What would you do for $5? Can this be a good source of leads or even a good publicity stunt for your biz?

Fangager.com: Reward your fans and followers with points for interacting with you socially online.

Groupme.com: Send group texts.

Resource page: 101FreeMarketing.com

Do you have any to add to the list? Visit the resource page and tell us what you think.

# Bonus Chapter

# CHAPTER 102

# A LOVE OF LEARNING AS A FREE MARKETING SKILL

For most of us, when the topic of learning or education comes up in conversation, we tend to gloss over and think of it as an activity that is boring and separate from the rest of our daily lives. Are you like that?

After all, most of us spent a significant portion of our youngest years getting up early in the morning and then going off to be educated. We couldn't wait for most days to end so we could stop being educated. How many people at your high school had to be dragged out of the building on the last day because they didn't want to leave?

Contrast that with the fact that I know of *no* successful marketers or business people that have a segmented view of education and learning. Instead we see everyday life with its successes, failures, and opportunities as an ongoing source of not just education and learning, but also for inspired creativity.

For example, it never fails that if I go to YouTube.com looking for advice on a specific topic, or even just to view a new video that someone has referred me to, I inevitably wind up finding other material that contains a marketing lesson for me. Even while watching television commercials I can learn a great deal about marketing if I pay attention to the *words* and *images* that are being used by an industry that pours billions of dollars into researching which words and images work best.

When it comes to being a successful marketer, your greatest asset is your own creativity. The most creative people that I know are the ones that constantly find new ways to surround themselves with interesting content, people that don't always agree with them, and ideas that come from a worldview different from their own.

**Be learning and taking notes always. Here are a few ideas on how to do this:**

- Keep a notebook near you at all times or make notes on your cell phone, or use a tool called EverNote.com that allows you to remember everything by storing notes you take from any device all in one online cloud.
- When watching TV or listening to advertising of any kind, jot down the power words you hear.
- Take note of the headlines used by successful online marketers. A good marketer spends most of their time on the headline, and only a portion of their time on the copy.
- When a story moves or inspires you, take note of where you heard it and the names involved. Recount the story with accuracy by simply flipping out your cell phone.
- Stop by Amazon.com from time to time and take note of the bestselling books overall and in your niche market. What ideas does that give you?
- Have a list of power players that you know could help take you to the next level in your business. Follow what projects they are working on, and use Google Alerts to track their progress. Support them in their efforts. This will force you to learn the skills that you need to continue to move up.
- Spend time every day doing things for people that can't do anything for you in return. The benefits are immeasurable. You'll be creating fans of your business, lifelong loyal supporters, and simply be doing what is right. Take note of the impact this activity has on you. When you have a slow or a down day, flip back through the stories of the reactions and responses you got by being a giver.
- Capture images and quotes that inspire you. Put hundreds of these on your computer screen saver. About 80 percent of the over 1,000 pictures that scroll through my screen-saver monitor are pictures of my family and friends. The rest are great quotes, scriptures, images of inspirational places, fascinating creations, and art. It's great to be randomly greeted with greatness every time I step into my office.

Never stop learning.
Never stop giving.
Never stop creating.
The world needs what you have to offer.
Please share it with us!

# ACKNOWLEDGMENTS

These are some of the most giving and inspirational people I've had the pleasure of learning from.

My wife Andrea Cockrum, who has stood by me and believed in me every day since we first met in 1992. Your creative spirit fills our home and shines in all you do.

For Chase, Trey, Tye, Zane, and Princess Aven. My kids are a gift from God and they inspire me daily.

My parents, Russ and Judy, who always encouraged me to pursue my dreams and have inspired my entrepreneurial spirit.

Perhaps no one better helped me define business success and balance in life better than my mentor since college, Bruce Beck. Thank you for everything. We miss Jennifer with you every day.

Kevin Ramsby. Thanks for writing the foreword for this book. More importantly thanks for showing us all exactly what it looks like when you stare fear in the face and show God's love in spite of it. Please read Kevin's incredible story at HopeVillageDetroit.com.

My creative, motivating, and uncompromising OfflineBiz.com partner, Andrew Cavanagh, who has been a part of the success of so many people.

Ron Cloer has contributed creativity and support to so many of the projects I've been a part of, including MySilentTeam.com, which was his idea. Thanks for the great work.

All the members of OfflineBiz.com and MySilentTeam.com that have made those two sites into two of the most dynamic and exciting communities online. I appreciate each of you (although I can't possibly list all 13,000+ of you!)

Thanks to Mike Koenigs and his creative team, who have supplied many of the tools that have made my online efforts (and the efforts of countless others) a huge success.

David Frey, Marlon Sanders, Seth Godin, and the other marketing geniuses that helped turn this marketing newbie into a confident marketing machine. I've learned so much from each of you.

John Jonas has been a great partner at OfflineBiz.com and he is a master of finding outsource partners for nearly any project. Thanks for the partnership.

Jim Orr has inspired more people than he knows, including me. You were a dedicated student and now you've become an invaluable partner.

Nathan Bailey has helped run my coaching business for a long time and he keeps getting better and better. Thanks for the loyalty and great work.

Nancy Alexander battled circumstances, health issues, and challenges that few understand and did what she could to establish herself and her business online. Your story has encouraged so many, including me. I'm honored to include your story in this book.

Dave Roever served his country bravely and has the scars to prove it, but there isn't a single scar on his heart. You've inspired millions including me.

Mike LeMoine started out as a reader and student of mine but has gone on to be a humble leader in the world of Internet marketing. Thanks for your loyalty and partnership at OfflineBiz.com.

Thanks to all of the many expert contributors at MySilentTeam.com. You've made it one incredible website! Thanks to Brigham Budd, John Bullard Jr., Lynn Dralle, Rob Frechette, Terry Gibbs, Dave Guindon, Avril Harper, Nathan Holmquist, Jenni Hunt, Kevin Johnson, James J. Jones, Tony Laidig, Steve Lindhorst, Barbara Ling, Andrew Lock, Dave Lovelace, Ben Mannino, Dave Espino, Skip McGrath, Ian McIntosh, Lee McIntyre, Julie Anna Schultz, Kristine McKinley, Rhea Perry and her son Drew, Fred Pineiro, John Thornhill, Stuart Turnbull, Robbin Tungett, and Julia Wilkinson. I'm blessed to have such great people behind me who are setting good examples in the IM industry.

Thea Woods responded quickly to my request on Facebook for a freehand artist. You did a great job on the illustrations for this book! Thank you.

Thanks to Richard Narramore, Linda Indig, and Lydia Dimitriadis at John Wiley & Sons for their patience and support in making this book happen. Thanks also to Jonathan Rozek who introduced me to the fine folks at John Wiley & Sons in late 2010.

# INDEX